EFFORTLESS MASTERY

LIBERATING THE
MASTER MUSICIAN WITHIN

BOOK AND CD
BY
KENNY WERNER

COVER DESIGN BY
ROBBIE ALTERIO

Published by
JAMEY AEBERSOLD JAZZ, INC.
P.O. Box 1244
New Albany, IN 47151-1244

www.jazzbooks.com

ISBN 1-56224-003-X

Dedication

For my father, who said that he loved to give advice and always wanted to write a book entitled <u>If I Were You!</u>

For my mother, who exemplifies selfless service and never offered me anything but encouragement.

For my beautiful daughter Katheryn — may her brashness never be thwarted.

For my wife Lorraine, who has taught me the meaning of Dharma, or righteous action — one of the most soulful and selfless people I've ever met. We're all lucky to have her!

Acknowledgements

I would like to thank the following people and institutions for helping make this book a reality:

Robin Brisker, for helping me figure out the early version of the cover design; Scott Reeves, for an early editing of the text; and Tony Moreno, for giving me much source material which I used extensively – all done as a labor of love.

The Danish Musician's Union and Jens Søndergaard, for inviting me to give a very special clinic on a "sunny day" in Copenhagen. The original text was an unedited transcription of my two days there.

Winnie and Eigil Mollsgaard, for allowing us to use their beautiful home for the clinic.

All the music societies and universities that invited me to give lectures and perfect my "schtick."

Jamey Aebersold, for immediately sharing my enthusiasm for this project, and for his own dedication to spirit.

For my beloved teacher,
Gurumayi Chidvilasananda,
for continually leading me along the
path towards the heart and reminding me
about "the inner music."

Selected Discography

As Leader:

Ken Werner Plays the Music of Bix Beiderbecke, Duke Ellington, James P. Johnson and George Gershwin: (Finnadar Records)

Beyond the Forest of Mirkwood: Ken Werner (Enja Records)*

298 Bridge St.: Ken Werner Sextet - Joe Lovano, Bill Drewes, Bill DeArango, Ratzo Harris, Tom Rainey (AMF Records)*

Kenny Werner: Introducing the Trio: Ken Werner Trio - Ratzo Harris, Tom Rainey (Sunnyside Records)*

Uncovered Heart: Ken Werner Sextet - Joe Lovano, Randy Brecker, Eddie Gomez, John Riley, Edson Cafe Adasilva (Sunnyside Records)*

Press Enter: Ken Werner Trio - Ratzo Harris, Tom Rainey (Sunnyside Records)*

Meditations: Ken Werner (SteepleChase Records)*

Copenhagen Calypso: solo (SteepleChase Records)

Gu-Ru: Ken Werner Trio - Ratzo Harris, Tom Rainey (TCB Records)*

Paintings: Ken Werner, Tom Rainey, Ratzo Harris, Billy Drewes, Tim Hagans, Mark Feldman, Eric Friedlander, Cafe Edson Adasilva, Jamie Haddad, Judith Silvano, Richard Martinez (Pioneer LDC, Inc., Japan)*

Kenny Werner Live at Maybeck Hall: Chris Potter and Ken Werner (Concorde Records)*

Kenny Werner Trio Live At Visiones: Tom Rainey, Ratzo Harris (Concorde Records)*

A Delicate Balance: Ken Werner Trio featuring Dave Holland and Jack DeJohnette (RCA/BMG)*

As Sideman:

Something Like A Bird: Charles Mingus (Atlantic Records)

I Know About the Life: Archie Shepp (SteepleChase Records)

Comin' and Goin': Jim Pepper (Europa Records)

Soul Song: Archie Shepp (Enja Records)*

Tangents: Chico Freeman (Elektra-Asylum Records)*

Twenty Years at the Village Vanguard: Mel Lewis Jazz Orchestra (Atlantic Records)

Tones, Shapes, and Colors: Joe Lovano (Soul Note Records)*

Transition: Peter Erskine (Denon Records)*

The Good Life: Archie Shepp (Varrick Records)

<u>Soft Lights and Hot Music:</u> Mel Lewis Jazz Orchestra (Music Masters Records)*

<u>To You:</u> Mel Lewis Jazz Orchestra (Music Masters Records)*

<u>Definitive Thad Jones:</u> Mel Lewis Jazz Orchestra (Music Masters Records)

<u>Definitive Thad Jones, Volume 2:</u> Mel Lewis Jazz Orchestra (Music Masters Records)

<u>Lost Art:</u> Mel Lewis Sextet (Music Masters Records)* **

<u>Confidential:</u> Special EFX (GRP Records)

<u>Street Talk:</u> Eddie Gomez (Columbia Records)

<u>Music Inside:</u> Joyce (Verve Forecast Records)

<u>Landmarks:</u> Joe Lovano (Blue Note Records)

<u>Sweet Soul:</u> Peter Erskine (BMG)*

<u>Language & Love:</u> Joyce (Verve Forecast Records)

<u>Reaching For the Moon:</u> Roseanne Vitro (CMG)*

<u>Global Village:</u> Special EFX (GRP Records)

<u>Sail Away:</u> Tom Harrell (Musidisc Records)

<u>Zounds:</u> Lee Konitz (Soul Note Records)*

<u>Universal Language:</u> Joe Lovano (Blue Note Records)

<u>Labyrinth:</u> Tom Harrell (RCA/BMG)

<u>Celebrating Sinatra:</u> Joe Lovano (Blue Note Records)

<u>Between Heaven and Earth:</u> Andy Stattman (Shanachie Records)

Betty Buckley:
 – <u>Children Will Listen</u> (Sterling Records)**
 – <u>With One Look</u> (Sterling Records)**
 – <u>The London Concert</u> (Sterling Records)***
 – <u>Live At Carnegie Hall</u> (Sterling Records)***
 – <u>Much More</u> (Sterling Records)**

  * *indicates original composition(s) recorded on this album*
 ** *indicates: Producer and arranger Kenny Werner*
*** *indicates: Arranger Kenny Werner*

PUBLISHED ARTICLES:

"Channeling Music." <u>Organica,</u> Spring 1988

"Play for the Right Reasons." <u>Organica,</u> Winter 1990

"Hostile Triads." <u>The Piano Stylist & Jazz Workshop,</u> April-May 1991

How To Use The CD

The exercises on the CD are basically meditations/ visualizations. Their purpose is to help you experience your "inner space." This is a state discussed in great detail throughout the book. The meditations are also featured as chapters in this book. When you reach those chapters, you will be instructed to listen to the corresponding exercise on the CD. Part of their effect is to relax and focus you after you have absorbed a great deal of information, and to give you a sense of the consciousness being described. If you listen to the meditations consecutively, they may sound repetitious as they contain much overlapping information. If used when indicated, however, they can enhance the experience of this book greatly.

I recommend that you carefully read the meditations presented in the chapters, as well as listening to them on the CD. In some cases, there are a few ideas in the chapters that are not mentioned on the CD.

After you have experienced the exercises the first time in their intended places, feel free to use any or all of them as an ongoing practice for contacting, working with and creating from that "inner space."

Some of the material in this book is specifically directed towards musicians and may seem highly technical, especially some of the examples in the chapter, "Step Four." Please feel free to pass over those passages. The bulk of the text should relate to anyone who aims to attain mastery in any area of their lives.

Table of Contents

Effortless Mastery

TRUTH: INNOVATION *IS JAZZ!*

Louis Armstrong, Duke Ellington, Bix Biederbecke,
Fats Waller, James P. Johnson, Jelly Roll Morton,
Scott Joplin, Charlie Parker, Dizzy Gillespie, Miles Davis,
Bud Powell, Bill Evans, Ornette Coleman,
Thelonious Monk, John Coltrane.
Can we agree that this is a fair representation
of the tradition of jazz?
What do these people all have in common?

THEY WERE ALL INNOVATORS!

INNOVATION IS THE TRADITION

Preface

$\mathcal{T}$he realm of the gifted has always seemed to be an exclusive club. The common belief is that, "Some of us have it, some of us don't." Implicit in that statement is the assumption that "most of us don't." The way music (and, I suspect other subjects as well) is traditionally taught works for those who "have it." Only very gifted or advanced students absorb the language of music in the way it is usually taught. Perhaps two percent of all music students ever attain anything. Many others struggle with the various elements of playing or improvising and as a result do not become performers.

Most people fall by the wayside. We don't seem to have given much thought to this discrepancy, simply accepting the old adage, "some of us have it and some of us don't." In cultures less intruded upon by "civilization," everyone is a musician. It has much to do with how music is introduced into our lives. This book will look at that subject and offer hope as well as practices to those who think they "don't have it." These practices will also increase the effectiveness of those who believe they do.

My belief is that, if you can talk, you can play. There are many reasons why the so-called less gifted don't get it. There are also methods of obtaining "it," which this book will discuss.

Many people have what I call musiphobia: fear of playing music. To a person afflicted with musiphobia, touching an instrument is like touching a hot stove. This is irrational, since one cannot get burned touching an instrument-yet it is a common problem. Though there are absolutely no negative consequences, most of us are afraid. It is not our fault. We have been programmed to *fear playing*. All too often, our relationship to music is doomed to failure.

A person might give up playing for reasons of insufficient talent, when upon closer inspection it becomes clear that the problem was the mode of study, or the lack thereof.

Many people are crippled by an inability to focus and by a sense of being overwhelmed. These problems are often mistaken for laziness or lethargy. There is a grand paradox in why we can't focus. This subject will be explored and many other paradoxes as well.

The exercises will help people on different levels in different ways. For example, there are good players who, for some reason, have little impact when they play. Everything works fine. They are "swinging" and all that, but still, something is not landing in the hearts of their audience. They are trapped in their minds. There is no nectar, because they are merely plotting and planning an approach along acceptable, "valid" lines of jazz style. The same thing commonly occurs to classical performers. They don't know what "channeling creativity" is because they, too, are dominated by their conscious minds. One must practice surrendering control to a larger, or higher force. It's scary at first, but eventually liberating. In Sanskrit the word is *moksha,* which means liberation. *Moksha* is attainable through the surrender of the small self to the larger "Self." I will introduce exercises for achieving that goal in music. After one taste of *moksha* through the medium of music, one will never want to return to a life of "thinking music." As one moves beyond the acceptable to the inevitable, creativity flows. Personal power will increase manyfold.

One truth for all players to contemplate is this: *learning new kinds of sophisticated jazz theory is not necessarily the key to freedom.* Once new theory is mastered, it is recited with the same dreary predictability as the old. If you are inhibited playing with the toys you have now, you will not play differently with new toys. Also, many jazz players feel that there is an experience in improvisation that they are not having, or not having fully enough. Classical musicians also report a "dryness" in their renderings of the great composers. It's like the priest who secretly has no love for God. The customs are observed, but there is no

10

true feeling. If the lamp is not lit, music can be as dreary as anything else. Along with the desire for a deeper experience comes an intense drive to be a better player. These aspects often work against each other. True musical depth is not about better playing, but about more "organic" playing.

It's very hard to let go in the combat of performance, but the exercises here will help you expand your "intuitive self." Over time, this intuition will emerge naturally without sabotaging the technical part of your performance. Assimilation into the whole is very much about "forgetting" one's self.

People who meditate or do tai chi will recognize many of the principles in this text. Even to them, it may be a revelation to know that one can live in the meditative state while playing an instrument. The mind is the chief culprit in most playing problems, and so any discipline that aims to control the mind is complementary to the process described here. Music can shoot through the musician like lightning through the sky if that music is unobstructed by thoughts. Therefore, the elimination of thoughts is a very relevant issue.

To dysfunctional learners, of which there are many in the jazz educational system, these exercises will cut through loads of books and exercises. It will help them get in touch with the next step in their development, putting aside all the theories, politics and fashions and instead focusing on their lives and the personal meaning that music has for them. In many cases, the decision to *study* music has robbed them of the ability to *play* music. They have lost respect for music that comes from within because they have been programmed to feel "unworthy." Some parts of this book will help these individuals get back to loving and honoring themselves, *with or without music!* Even many great professionals suffer from low self esteem and other negative illusions.

For those who practice things that never surface in their playing, (and there are many such musicians), I offer reasons for why this happens, as well as a way out of this dilemma. This book also contemplates the relationship of belief systems to effectiveness and how we "practice for mediocrity."

In addition this book delves into the nature of artistry, and quite extensively into the nature of mastery. I will discuss how to effortlessly play what you already know and reach a depth you didn't think you were capable of.

There are certainly artists who can enjoy music in a positive way, artists who always know how to become inspired and how to execute effortlessly. But the percentage of people who do this is small. Much of this book is for those who are not succeeding in their efforts to fulfill their hopes and dreams musically, and for musicians who feel tense and constricted while playing. Some of the ideas contained here are radical. They challenge institutions to change and individuals to move from the comfort zone of limitation and blossom into their higher selves. If you've been playing for thirty years and hardly ever enjoyed it, if you've constantly pointed to other players and thought that they possessed something you didn't, or if you've practiced for years and never really improved, read on.

Chapter 1
Introduction

$\mathcal{T}$here is an ocean. It is an ocean of consciousness, an ocean of bliss. Each one of us is a drop in that ocean. In that sense, we are all one — or as a famous American television commercial states, "We're all connected." Illusion would have us think that we are all separate entities, separate drops. But if that were true, we would all evaporate rather quickly.

As we expand our limited selves into this infinite consciousness, we tap into a network of infinite possibilities, infinite creativity — great, great power. Carried by the waves of this ocean, we swirl past all limitations and maximize our God-given potential. Everything good that can possibly happen to us, from within and without, does. Our abilities expand beyond all reasonable limits, and we become a magnetic force for abundant light and all that that implies.

We are all part of a universal game. Returning to our essence while living in the world is the object of the game. The earth is the game board, and we are the pieces on the board. We move around and around until we remember who we really are, and then we can be taken off the board. At that point, we are no longer the game-piece, but the player; we've won the game.

As musicians/healers, it is our destiny to conduct an inward search, and to document it with our music so that others may benefit. As they listen to the music coming through us, they too are inspired to look within. Light is being transmitted and received from soul to soul. Gradually, the planet moves from darkness to light. We as musicians must surrender to the ocean of our inner selves. We must descend deep into that ocean while the sludge of the ego floats on the surface. We let go of our egos and permit the music to come through us and do its work. We act as the instruments for that work.

If we can live in this realization, we will constantly have deep motivation for what is played, never getting stuck in the ungrateful consciousness of good gigs/bad gigs, out-of-tune pianos, low fees, ungracious audiences, and so on. Instead, our minds will be consumed with what a very great privilege it is to be the one selected to deliver the message to others. We will no longer be caught in the mundane world of good music/bad music ("am I playing well?") Instead, our hearts and minds will be focused on the task of remaining empty and alert to receiving this God-inspired information and translating it faithfully, without any coloration from us.

Chapter 2

My Story

Numb in Long Island

I grew up in a cultural wasteland. I'm sure that people from the suburbs all across America can identify. Post-World War II America had witnessed "miraculous" innovations, such as television, drug-induced labor and TV dinners. The baby boom was such that hospitals came to rely on drugs to hurry along the process of birth; no time for mom to get too comfy. Machines monitored expectant mothers. Caesarean births increased greatly. Drugs and intrusive hospital procedures – such as treating the mothers-to-be as if they were sick – severed the time-honored process of mother-child bonding. If Mary had given birth to Jesus in 1950, all those Madonna pictures would have shown her groggy from drugs with an insert of Jesus under a heat lamp next to twenty-five babies!

This time period produced "amazing discoveries." Cans and boxes were created to preserve food: just heat and serve. Researchers found ways of adding vitamins and minerals to create a "superior product." Fortune smiled on our civilization, and flavor-enhancers were born! I ate canned peaches packed in delicious sugar gravy for about fifteen years before actually eating a fresh peach. What a disappointment that was! Fresh peaches tasted like lemon-flavored suede shoes! Nothing could match the ecstasy of drinking the juice from canned peaches or pears.

Most of the kids I knew ate dinner the same way; we took our plates from our moms and went to the den to eat alone while watching television. In that way, we could remain blissfully shut down. Television short-circuited our minds, and the salt and sugar in all the food kept our senses occupied. By eating alone, wn didn't have to converse or answer questions. There was enough distasteful stuff of that kind in school.

I'm waiting for new, startling evidence to turn up, showing that the Greeks and Romans had a crude form of television before their downfall. Television and its programing contributes more to the dehumanization of society than any other development in history. It seems that the successful strategy in the market place is to keep us hungry, horny, and as unfocused as possible. Mind-melding with TV robs us of an inner connection and makes living in the moment intolerable. TV is a drug, and we as a nation have become hooked. It isn't hard to see why the baby-boomers pursued their drugs so vigorously. Turn on Saturday morning TV for kids and watch an ad for cereal! Beams of light come streaming out of the box, and when the cereal is consumed, the child becomes encircled in golden honey light and then blasts off for Venus! Jimi Hendrix and Janis Joplin died trying to feel that good!

School was a place where we were all supposed to develop our minds and learn social interaction. Whatever personal interests we were developing dissolved in an ocean of useless information. Since the relevant was indistinguishable from the irrelevant, it was hard to develop a genuine affinity for things we might have cared about. For me, there was no joy, just homework. Studying music in elementary school was as interesting as a lecture on early menopause. The teachers in my time were likely to subvert a child's wonder about the nature of sound and its formation into music. Music became another thing you had to pay attention to: more questions to answer, more tests to take, more scolding to incur, more *pressure*. Teachers often didn't relay the information with any enthusiasm. In school, we were asked to care about things we didn't care about and stop caring about the things we did, and generally behave in a manner that contradicted childhood. We were fed to institutions who baby-sat us, when it was love and compassion that we craved. I understand that it is much better in many schools these days, but the education I grew up with was of the conveyor-belt variety. Our society was — and still is — the progenitor of prepackaged emotions, fast-food boredom, "popping fresh" apathy, artistic oblivion, pop culture body-snatchers — or, as Robert Hughes puts it, living in "the empire of Donald Duck."[1]

No wonder Western civilization is producing so few real artists. In American society, a child is lucky to survive with his or her artistic tendencies intact (or unlucky, perhaps?)

School Daze

In school, I had a tendency to daydream. I would sit in class, hum to myself and look out the window. Whatever the teacher was saying dissolved into a non-linguistic drone. Having no interest in what was taught, I could not concentrate. Extremely bored, I learned to be anywhere but in the moment!

By junior high school, I was a solidly dysfunctional learner; one of many such casualties. For example, I remember taking a class in algebra. The first week or two, I was involved in the subject. But one day, I missed five minutes of what the teacher was saying and was lost for the rest of the semester. Ashamed by this, I would keep quiet. I developed a belief system of personal inadequacy. The same thing happened with most of my courses. After a few minutes of not understanding anything, my mind would drift and I would space out. Everything got kind of surreal. Once in a while, I would try to tune in, but it seemed that the teacher was no longer speaking English. His or her mouth would be moving, but the sound coming out was "wawawawawa ... "

As I hid my ignorance day after day, the fire of low self-esteem raged, and with it, the steam of escapism rose within me. I would escape this self-loathing by absorbing myself in television when I got home. My mind was quieted by the blue light as I stimulated my senses with sugar. Later on in life, I would find much more dynamic substances with which to stuff my feelings. In this way, the trials and failures of the day would drift into distant memory

---

[1]Hughs Robert. *The Culture of Complaint*

— not to disappear, but to arrange themselves as another piece in the mosaic of my dysfunctional existence. It wasn't until very much later in life, while in therapy, that I heard the word "dysfunctional." After being told I was dysfunctional, I remember leaving the therapist's office elated. I wanted to celebrate! No wonder nothing ever worked. I wasn't a "bad" person, I just wasn't functioning correctly. What a relief!

As a child, toward the end of the day I would have gotten nothing done—no homework, no practicing, nothing. I remember my father coming down the stairs from his nap at 5:00 pm (he worked nights) and asking menacingly, "Did Kenny practice?" My mom would say, "No, not yet." He would look down at me in the den watching television and point his finger, saying something sternly to me. I don't remember what it was, I was so busy cringing!

I would go to sleep having made a resolution to start the next day off better. But the next day I would get overwhelmed, and the whole dysfunctional process would begin again. I thought, in my self-loathing, that I was lazy and stupid. Mental hell on earth is waking up with expectations every morning and going to sleep disappointed in yourself every night!

Most Popular Guy

I had a free ride of sorts. Although I had very little success scholastically, I had even less athletically. I was a total couch potato and suffered from great lethargy. In the summer, when all the kids would go to camp or elsewhere, I would stay in the house next to the air conditioner. The TV and refrigerator kept me company all summer. I felt isolated and numb. I was the only kid who came back from summer vacation with his skin paler than when school had ended!

I had no outstanding physical attributes, nothing that distinguished me from the other students. I would have been a total loser in school but for one thing—I could play the piano. And I could play very well. I started playing at seven, and by eight, I was playing for assembly. At nine years old I was playing gigs.

I made absolutely no impression on my fellow students until I would sit down to play. Then the world changed completely. I was it: Mr. "Bad" himself! The athletes, who otherwise didn't know I existed, suddenly put their arms around me and proclaimed me their friend. The greasers (motorcycle types) would just as soon beat me up as talk to me, but if I played a tune they liked, they became my protectors. ("Don't mess with my brother Kenny — or *I'll kill you!*"). The girls — oh how I wanted them to notice me! They could be very cruel. But if I was in the middle of the party cranking something out on the piano, there would always be that one special girl who would emerge with a soulful smile and tell me how much she loved my playing. That was okay with me, as long as I was loved and admired for something!

I was the best player wherever I went. This masked my despair and self-loathing. I depended heavily on my playing for a sense of self-worth. Playing the music came so easily to me that it was hard for people to believe that I was malfunctioning. If I was failing at everything else, it was okay because people could point to the way I played, as if to say that I was all right. I even felt guilty and loathsome for the free ride.

Miles Who?

My musical influences at that time were primarily TV themes and music from movies I watched on TV. After that, they were AM radio, where pop music was played in those days, and Broadway show tunes. As a pianist, I was influenced by the records of Roger Williams playing *Rhapsody In Blue* and Andre Previn playing jazz arrangements of *My Fair Lady*. My father had bought me a Fats Waller album when I was younger. That and the Previn album were the only contacts I had with jazz. I played bastardized stride piano because of hearing Waller and a friend of my father who used to come over to our house and play piano. In junior high school a friend played the John

Coltrane record "My Favorite Things" for me, and I hated it. My attention span was far too short for that music, and to my ears, there was no melody. Even today when I am asked who my influences were, I usually answer Chico Marx, Jimmy Durante, and Victor Borge (the latter two had TV shows, you know).

Suicide Watch at The Manhattan School of Music

Musically, everything was under control. I seemed to be getting something for nothing until the day of reckoning came. I applied and was accepted to Manhattan School of Music as a classical piano major. It didn't matter that I didn't know Beethoven from Brahms, or that *I didn't care to know*. I was going to be a concert pianist!

Up to this time music had been a free ride. Without practicing at all, I was the best player everywhere I went. The messages I received from parents, aunts, uncles, and teachers were "You're great" and "We'll see you in Carnegie Hall!" Because of these messages and the extreme low self-esteem I had in all other areas, I thought that I had to be nothing less than the best. I felt as though my life would truly be a failure if I didn't play at Carnegie Hall one day.

I was always either very high or very low. When I would hear a pianist play better than me, *I would want to die!* I would literally feel worthless. I had come to depend so heavily on my talent for validation that I couldn't face not being God's gift to music.

Manhattan School of Music was a real slap in the face. There were students with talent equal to mine, but they could practice long hours. I was devastated. Instead of being the special one — the musician — I was, for the first time in my life, just another musician, and not a particularly distinguished one at that. I felt like an impostor: someone who only pretended to be involved in what he was doing. Without the distinction of being that special guy, I was nothing. I had no purpose, no direction. I didn't even know why I was playing music anymore.

A New Beginning

Although life didn't really feel worth living, I didn't have the courage to end it, although the thought of ending it made me feel vaguely peaceful. I had heard that Berklee School of Music had a good jazz program. I didn't know much about jazz, but I did know that it involved improvisation, which was all that I ever really loved about music. Lord knows that if there were any glimpses of my inner self in those early years, they came when I sat down at the piano with no plan in mind — no form, no structure, just my raw feeling and a few friendly listeners. (I always had to have listeners. Otherwise, it wasn't worth giving up valuable TV time.)

When I enrolled in Berklee, I was delighted to find other misfits like myself, people who truly didn't know where they were at or what they were doing. These guys became my fraternity. I responded to this new, stimulating environment by having the first B-plus year of my life. I actually made the dean's list — and I was practicing! Praise the Lord, I was practicing! It felt great. It all related to improvising, so I guessed I was in the right place.

I began to really appreciate jazz and all its great artists. For the next few years, I tried to do what most music students do: imitate the masters, not only in playing, but in mind and speech. I lamented my Jewishness, the fact that I came from Long Island. When people asked, I just said that I was from New York.

Most of my friends were concerned with learning the language of jazz without sacrificing individuality. Unfortunately, this prevented some of them from adequately learning the language (a problem that I'll address in a later chapter). But while I was there, I met a few people who would help shape my future. The seeds were planted for what would become my path.

Madame Chaloff

People were telling me about a legend whom many great

pianists were supposed to have studied with in Boston. Madame Chaloff was a mystical figure who taught the "secret of music." I found her to be a truly light-filled being.

She was about eighty years old when I met her, but her hair was golden reddish blond and seemed to glow as if a little spotlight were following her around the room. She spoke of the secret of playing piano. It had to do with the pianist's arms "defying gravity." We worked on other physical actions as well. We even worked on how my walking could be more graceful.

She taught the perfect way to drop a finger. This was my first introduction to effortlessness. Until then, I had grunted and groaned and made all sorts of weird faces. People loved the faces I made, because it meant that I was really into the music. I later recognized this as tension and nothing more. Madame Chaloff was a real stickler for the perfect drop of the finger. I spent months learning to play one note. I think that once or twice I got it right, and we actually went on to the second finger!

Madame Chaloff was very one-pointed in her focus. Music was about playing for God. I was grateful for that message, because I had been trying to meditate under the tutelage of a popular guru at the time. She made the connection for me between spirit and music. Through her, I was able to merge the two. I would often go to the lessons with my own agenda, bringing so many questions. But once in her chamber, I would enter another dimension. Everything that seemed important would dissolve. I felt as if in the presence of truth. I know that this experience was true for many others as well, though not for all.

At one point, it had been a while since I had seen her, and I had drifted off her subtle path. After a distressing breakup with my longtime girlfriend, I was so distraught that I decided to see Madame Chaloff. I thought, "This time she'll see the pain I'm in and really want to listen to my sad story. Maybe it would be good if I were crying when she came to the door. Yes! That's a very good idea! I'll cry, and she'll see that I don't need that spiritual stuff right now, and she'll comfort me and pity me and give me solace." I got to her door, sad-faced and ready for sympathy. As she opened the door, I involuntarily smiled. She took one look at me and asked, "Where have you been? Come on in here. We've got a lot of work to do!" And we went right to it.

I must regretfully say that I never did learn to play that one note right. It was too early for me to learn that lesson. I had the urgency and ambition of a typical college student. Her message was too high for me. When I was with her, I knew I was hearing truth, but I would lose it soon after leaving. I must have been meant to learn this truth, however, because the next place I moved to, another teacher was waiting to show me the very same thing.

João Assis Brasil

After attending Berklee on and off for three years, I got the opportunity to go to Rio de Janeiro. João Assis Brasil was a concert pianist who happened to be the twin brother of the late saxophonist Victor Assis Brasil, with whom I traveled to Rio to play concerts.

João was entering European competitions and practicing eight hours a day. He had achieved a high degree of excellence through intense pressure and practice. The result was a nervous breakdown. He returned home to live with his parents and went to therapy five days a week. He started to practice two things that would restore him to health.

Whenever his mind tormented him, his therapist told him to go somewhere and chant, "I must be kind to myself, I must be kind to myself!" He practiced that and a simple exercise that a teacher in Vienna had shown him: a five-finger exercise that consisted of releasing the fingers effortlessly, one by one, onto the keyboard. This was similar to Madame Chaloff's one-finger exercise, but not as elusive. This exercise only needed to be done for five minutes — a short amount of time to focus without pressure. Concentrating in this manner, five minutes became ten, ten became twenty, and so on, until one could practice effortlessly for as long as one wanted. At the time I met him,

João had been recovering for about two years, and his personality was rather luminous. The therapy had helped him mentally, and using the five minute concept, he had built up his practice time to eight to ten hours a day. But now it was pressure-free, and he felt a great deal of love and joy while doing it. As I watched him play, I felt like some kind of inferior species — he made it all look so easy!

I was fortunate to live in that household for a couple of months. It gave me a unique opportunity to practice only from that space. João was going in the same direction as Madame, but he wasn't so removed from the problems of the mind. He had dealt with the same issues as I had and could address them for me.

For example, one day we were listening to Horowitz playing — I don't remember which piece, but João was joyously listening while I was biting my fingernails. I was thinking so much, I could barely hear the music. Thoughts like, "Oh, that playing is so great ... it's really painful to hear it! ... This means that I am nothing ... unless ... if I practice eight hours a day for the next twenty years..." raced through my mind. My mind often behaved like that. In fact, it behaved that way all the time. Just at that moment, João put his hand on my shoulder, and I jumped. He startled me! When I turned around, he was smiling. He must have been reading my mind, or at least my body language, because he said, "BE KIND TO YOURSELF!" This statement, uttered at that moment, was revelatory. It showed me the folly of my thoughts. At that moment, I was able to let go, and suddenly I HEARD THE MUSIC! Horowitz was playing so exquisitely! I felt reborn (at least temporarily). I was sitting there enjoying the music for the first time as a listener rather than a compulsive musician, one whose self-worth was on the line every time he heard someone else play well. I became aware of what was wrong with me. This was a key lesson about myself.

The five-finger exercise that João gave me seemed simple enough. I only had to practice for five minutes. As a dysfunctional learner and undisciplined person, that sounded great. But the assignment at first terrified me. He wanted me to practice nothing but the five-finger exercise for two weeks! I was to do absolutely no other playing. I could observe the panic in my mind and the illusions it was creating. I thought that in two weeks, I would forget how to play. Even more absurd was the notion that I would lose so much valuable practice time. What practice time? That was my problem to begin with: I never practiced!

With great trepidation, I began the exercise. Day after day, I noticed some good things. It occurred to me that, for the first time in my musical life, *I was actually doing the work assigned to me by a piano teacher!* It was so simple that I never felt overwhelmed. Five minutes seemed to be the right amount of time. One of the reasons I never practiced was the belief that I had to sit there for *five hours* for it to mean anything. Since I never had five hours free in any given day (too busy watching television, I guess) I never got around to practicing. Another reason I was now practicing was that the material was so simple: the effortless release of each finger to the key. Thumb to fifth finger and back; then the other hand; and then....finished! Just walk away! It had a very calming effect, cleansing me with a feeling of a new beginning. I felt really good.

I floated serenely through the days, just sitting down for a few minutes in the morning, afternoon, and night, feeling good about myself. I wish I could say that I made it through the whole two weeks without playing anything else, but after about six days, I played hooky. A beautiful Brazilian woman called one day to invite me and Victor to a party. She wanted us to play a duo. I told her that I was on a special program and not playing right now. But she asked me in that special way, and I acquiesced!

When we arrived at the party, people asked us to play. I apologized for what was about to happen. I explained that Victor's crazy brother had me touching the piano for only five minutes a day. I was out of shape and had no idea what would come out. What followed was something I will never forget. We played *Autumn Leaves*. I put my hands on the piano and *they played!* I mean that they actually played by themselves while *I watched!* And what they played was blowing my mind and everybody else's. Not only was it good, but it was so much better

25

than I usually played! The change was astounding. In just six days of meditating, more or less, at the piano, I was totally different! My touch, usually hard and strained, sounded balanced and beautiful, like Bill Evans. I had discovered the secret of his sound. Also, at this stage of my development, I usually needed about thirteen notes to find eight good ones. There was no great rhythm or symmetry to my lines. But this night, I was playing perfect, symmetrical lines in beautiful swinging time. And again, I must stress the point that I was *only observing, not doing!*

This powerful demonstration made a believer of me for life. I realized that the goal is letting go of my ego and being kind to myself, playing only what wants to come out effortlessly. I now knew that I could observe myself play and embrace the spiritual ideas of service and surrender. The pursuit of these ideals would stretch me further than my limited consciousness could ever do *and make me a better player!* This blew my mind.

I have since found confirmation of this process in many ancient spiritual traditions. Our society is very much in the dark as to what its spiritual purpose is, and our musicians no less so.

In the course of working with music students of all ages, from the amateur to the professional, I have found many sincere but ego-ridden musicians. As I was, they are defeated by self-centeredness, and lack vision and purpose. And, most important, they don't know what music is, who they are, and what they are really doing here.

Chapter 3
Why Do We Play?

*For people of my tribe, with its rich musical
context, exposure to music begins in the womb,
when pregnant mothers join in the community
dances. From inside the womb, our babies feel the
vibrations of the rhythms enter their bodies.
Infants are then wrapped onto their mothers' backs
with a cloth and taken into the dancing circle with
everyone else.*

Yayo Diallo[1]

Your First Time

I remember my first time. I went to a friend's birthday party
and his father played the piano for us. I was mesmerized. I had
never seen a piano played before. I ran home after the party
and told my mother that I wanted to play. "Get me a piano, will
ya, will ya, will ya?"

For Christmas they rented one with an option to buy. If I
took to it, they would buy it. I'll never forget the day it arrived.
I could hardly wait to touch it. I started to pick out the notes of
some songs I knew, and I remember running into the kitchen to
proudly exclaim to my mother, "Good news, mom. I won't be
needing any lessons. I've already figured out how to play!" I
believed myself to have been a musician from that time on ...

Why do we travel the sometimes masochistic route of
becoming a musician? Being an artist in "civilized" society doesn't
seem as secure as owning stock in IBM (though it may be no

---

[1]Hart, Mickey. *Planet Drum, A Celebration of Percussion and Rhythm.*
New York: Harper Collins, 1991.

less so). So what compels us to try? How did we become "co-
dependent" with music? We love it and can't leave it, no matter
how unsatisfied some of us are with the fruits of our efforts.
Why do we do it? Take a moment to contemplate *your* first time:

Think back to the time you first touched an instrument.
Remember the wondrous sound that came out? Think of that
virginal experience. Anything you played sounded incredible.
There was so much magic in the sound! You couldn't wait to do
it again. You probably didn't think there was anything to learn.
You were content to hear the sound come back to you. This was
the unfolding of a natural process.

Stimulated by the sound, your curiosity about music could
have grown from there. If you were left alone, you might have
developed various relationships to the different sounds on that
instrument. The different octaves, combinations of notes (if it
was polyphonic), loud and soft, and so on, would have expressed
something personal for you, something that "just wanted to come
through."

Perhaps we would have many more musical languages,
creative techniques, ways of playing the instruments and even
innovative fingerings if everyone had been left to their own
devices for the first few years with an instrument. If there were
no pressure to learn early on, kids might become curious about
how to find the songs they hear on the radio, develop a real
yearning to know harmony, and so on.

A friend of mine who is a painter told me that when she was
a child, she was trying to draw a bracelet on a wrist, but she
couldn't get the perspective right. The bracelet is not supposed
to be seen behind the wrist. After a long time, she became
frustrated and started to cry. Her mother came in and showed
her how to hide part of the bracelet behind the wrist, making it
look much more realistic. Her own experimentation had led her
to yearn for this knowledge, and her mother's teaching was right
on time. That lesson really stayed with her. Similarly, you would
have been excited to have a teacher come forward at the right
time and show you what you craved to know about music. It

would have been an artistic journey from the very beginning! But unfortunately most of us never traveled that road.

Education: The Death Knell

Usually, somebody comes along at an early stage and breaks the groove. A parent, for example, tells you things like, "You must have a teacher," or "Nothing will come of this if you don't practice." Even if that is true, the dreariness of this message drones on, and the magic evaporates. Perhaps that was not the *first thing* a child needs to know. Music has now been relegated to the maximum security prison of homework.

Many people I've talked with say that they studied an instrument at an early age but let it go in their teens. They always express regret that they didn't continue.

But why did they stop?

The answer is that the bliss of music had been filtered out of their studies. Teachers doled out their assignments with drab monotony. How could the teachers know the bliss that was there? Many of them had never experienced it growing up, either. Just as abused children become abusive parents, music teachers force-feed dry information from generation to generation. The dryness of music (as well as all other subjects) in school causes young people to tune out. It is no coincidence that they become rebellious teenagers, rejecting "rules" in favor of "fun." Music often gets identified with the rules instead of with "freedom" and "fun." When a kid gets serious about music, it is usually not the music he or she has been taught in school. However, I hear that the situation is improving in some public schools.

I used to love to play stick ball with my friends. We would play until it was so dark that we could hardly see the ball. I hated to come in to get my practicing done. That was no more inviting than doing my homework. I do not mean to blame teachers and parents for trying to do their jobs. But our educational system has not served our creativity very well. I don't profess to have the answers. I am just citing some of the reasons why an overwhelming amount of people lost their love of music through *studying it.* Later on, many regain it as listeners, and hence the common outcry, "I wish I'd never quit my piano lessons!"

Despite the odds, many of us who get bitten by the music bug stay with it. Those first experiences make music addicts out of us, and from then on we are driven. However, as we continue to pursue music, many other motivations become superimposed onto our pure love of playing.

Self-Worth

As you can see from my story, the quality of a person's playing can determine his or her self-worth. A feeling of little self-worth is very common in musicians, young and old alike, yielding unsatisfying results. It seems as if in order to be good you have to *play good.* Musicians who fall into this trap generally don't enjoy life. Every day brings anxiety. They are either elated or depressed. Each solo is the acid test of apparent worth. Their self-respect is more volatile than the stock market. They rarely play anything of depth. They are like the person who is always trying to get us to like him; we usually don't.

Fear of Failure

Many young people go to music school because they think that it's a great idea to be a jazz musician. However, once the decision is made, they dare not quit for fear of failing. They don't know what they're doing there, but they don't know what else to do. In time, most of these kids drop off.

If you think you might like to quit, *do it.* Don't worry about failing. You'd be a failure if you *didn't* quit! You might miss an opportunity in some other field. At Manhattan School of Music, I was afraid to quit because it would mean that I was a failure. It was obvious that I was no more suited to be a concert pianist than to be a nuclear physicist. Fear of failure blinded me from this fact, but only after I moved on did my life begin.

I'm Going To Be A Star!

This has got to be the craziest reason of all. Of all the people who pursue careers in music, be it jazz or classical (or playing weddings and barmitzvahs), how many become stars? A musician's life is the riskiest investment in the universe. If it's money you're after, become a bank president!

If you are a struggling musician-artist, there are only three real reasons you don't quit: 1) you're having a lot of fun and you love the music *THAT MUCH;* 2) you have a deep-seated need to express yourself through music; or 3) you are either too lazy, too scared, or too dysfunctional to retrain for another career. I believe that if you're motivated by either of the first two reasons, or by both, you will be taken care of.

Many of us are unaware of the depths that music beckons us to. Keith Jarrett, in an article for the New York Times, used the occasion of Miles Davis' death to comment on the music scene and society in general. He wrote, "Try to imagine the first musician. He was not playing for an audience, or a market, or working on his next recording, or touring with his show, or working on his image. He was playing out of need, out of his need for the music. Every year the number of musicians who remember why they play music in the first place gets smaller, and the greatest loss from this handful was Miles Davis, who died last year."[2]

In the movie, *The Piano,* Holly Hunter plays a mute who travels to another country to be wedded to a man she's never met. Without the ability to speak, she develops her "voice" playing the piano. Whenever she plays, she is drawn deep within and uplifted emotionally and spiritually. The piano is her rock, her center, her lover and her voice. Intoxicated by the sound, she has little patience for idle chatter. In such a person, the divine musician manifests, and nothing is wasted.

Keith Jarrett writes, "The original musician was not looking for his image; he was using his voice to learn about the world.

---

[2]Jarrett, Keith. New York Times Article

He knew the world to be liquid (i.e., not made up of discrete entities)." Jarrett decries the fact that "we see the world as 'bits of information,'" and laments that "fewer and fewer musicians let us know who they are by the expression of music."[3]

The Original Purpose

Let us remember that, in the beginning, music was our sole means of communication.

"A study of ancient traditions reveals that the first divine messages were given in song, as were the Psalms of David, the Song of Solomon, the Gathas of Zoroaster and the Gita of Krishna."[4] So writes Hazrat Inayat Khan, the great Sufi musician.

The original purpose of music was worship, divine intelligence, and basic communication. Music intoxicated the human soul. It was, according to ancient legend, the song of angels that induced the unwilling soul to enter the body of Adam. In every way, music is our bond between the material and the eternal.

"In the beginning of human creation, no language such as we now have existed, but only music. Man first expressed his thoughts and feelings by low and high, short and prolonged sounds. Man conveyed his sincerity, insincerity, disinclination, pleasure or displeasure by the variety of his musical expressions."[5]

Language is the retention of rhythm without pitch. In this way, poetry was born of music. Ancient spiritual texts were expressed in poetry such as the Vedas, Ramayana, Mahabaharata and the Bible.

Distilling poetry of its rhythm, we have prose. So it can be said that all language is derived from music. Music can put a baby to sleep or inspire a soldier in war.

[3]Jarrett, Keith. Ibid
[4]Hazrat Inayat Khan, *The Sufi Message* p. 51
[5]Ibid. p. 51

Our most natural tendency is to make music. It requires no more thought than breathing. "The infant begins his life on earth by moving its arms and legs, thus showing the rhythm of its nature, and illustrating the philosophy which teaches that rhythm is the sign of life."[6]

Actually, music is derived from sound, and sound is composed of vibration. Now we get to the heart of the matter, for all matter is made up of vibrations. It is a scientific fact that, although we see solids when we look at an object, what we are really seeing is fluid vibrations organized in sufficiently gross frequencies to form solid matter.

Hazrat Inayat Khan says: "The life absolute from which has sprung all that is felt, seen, and perceived, and into which all again merges in time, is a silent, motionless and eternal life .... Every motion that springs forth from this silent life becomes active in a certain part, and creates in every moment more and more activity, losing thereby the peace of the original silent life. It is the grade of activity of these vibrations that accounts for the various planes of existence .... The activity of vibrations makes them grosser, and thus the earth is born of the heavens."[7]

We are made up of vibrations. And thus, all things can be said to have music in them. It travels to us directly from the infinite on the wings of vibration and molds itself to our every desire. Sound, when seen in this way, is no less than a gift from God. "Music is the only means of understanding among birds and beasts."[8]

Music and art remain the best way we have to appreciate creation, hence, the Indian concept that man was created so that God could behold himself (or herself). This concept presents a magnificent image of humans as empty molds for God to pour consciousness into. When man expresses the inexpressible, he does so on the wings of song. The song evaporates somewhat as we stop hearing the inner voice. All music manifests from the

---

[6]Hazrat Inayat Khan, *The Sufi Message* p. 44
[7]Ibid p. 13
[8]Ibid p. 50

inner music: the "unstruck sound," as it were. The death-rattle of any religion may be heard in the absence of song and the increase of verbiage (and fund-raising).

Many of the world's indigenous musical traditions went beyond the point of surrender into trance. Religions were based entirely on music. Mickey Hart, of "The Grateful Dead" fame, wrote a beautiful book entitled *Planet Drum, A Celebration of Percussion and Rhythm.* Describing the shamans of West Africa and their function in society, he says that they are "professional trance travelers, handling the tribe's communication between this world and the spirit world. Shamans are the healers, psychics, weather workers; they lobby the higher powers to assure a good hunt. A shaman typically needs three things: power songs to summon his spirit allies, spirit allies to guide him to the world tree, and a drum to ride there on."[9]

Notice that in traveling to the "world tree," two out of the three things he needs have to do with music: a drum and a song.

The shaman's state is trance, a state that eludes most of us in the modern world, but which may still be witnessed in an inspired jazz soloist or classical performer.

Possession trance is a state where "the spirits ride the drumbeat down into the body of the trance-dancer."[10] Hart writes: "Scholars connect the West African possession cultures with the ancient Neolithic mother goddess culture that nine thousand years ago stretched from eastern Europe into what is now the Sahara desert. When the slave trade began in the seventeenth century, this technique of possession trance was carried to the New World. In those places where the Africans were allowed to keep their drums, it mutated into candomble, santeria, and vodun. In America, where the drums were prohibited for many generations, this legacy of possession-trance dance rhythm was

---

[9]Hart, Mickey. *Planet Drum, A Celebration of Percussion and Rhythm.*
  New York: Harper Collins, 1991.
[10]Ibid

shorn of its spiritual dimension, becoming instead jazz, blues, rhythm and blues, and rock and roll."[11]

This is a significant point, for it reveals the origin of jazz to be a "legacy of possession-trance dance rhythm shorn of its spiritual dimension."

These comments by Mickey Hart excited me because I have heard and read of great beings who have said many times that all search for sense pleasures is really the search for God. Even the conqueror in war — what is he looking for? No matter how much of the world he rules during his life, he will have to surrender it when he dies. So what is he really after? Although he doesn't realize it, he is seeking oneness with the self in all things. When a musician superficially craves security in the level of his playing, what is he really after? It is said that one drop of ecstasy tasted from the self, the God inside us, renders all other pursuits insignificant. At that point, the seeker has found everything he has sought. Every song is either praise or an entreatment for more connection with the beloved.

As enslaved peoples are separated from their religion, the lyrics of the song change. The cry is for sense pleasures: more sex, money, alcohol. How many blues and rock and roll songs speak about that? Desire for "my God" is supplanted by the desire for "my man." Mankind's vision decays, entangled by the search for temporary relief from its subjugation to false gods. But the cry is still there, even if man no longer knows for what. It is the yearning for unity, for oneness as experienced in the mother's womb, attuned to the rhythm of her heartbeat. The muffled song can still be heard from the God within "seeking to behold himself," and man's yearning to be one with him. Later, the blues, drained of all meaning, decays into a twelve-bar crossword puzzle to be "re-harmonized" in theory class. Finally, jazz visionaries revive it as an Indian Tala and ascend on its numeric highway.

---

[11] Ibid, 1991.

Chapter 4

Beyond Limited Goals

*E*ven in European classical music and American jazz, we can witness something akin to the trance state. Artists who can enter this state are the most focused performers, the most accomplished at what they do, and they usually give us the most memorable concerts. We can remember such concerts as being an "experience." Perhaps it is such an experience that compels us to become musicians; it can be that life-changing.

How does one achieve that level of musicianship — of *humanness?* How does one evolve into a riveting presence so worthy of praise? Limited goals, such as trying to impress people, find security, play "valid" jazz, and so on, block that goal. Surrender is the key, and the first thing to surrender is one of your most prized possessions: *YOUR OBSESSIVE NEED TO SOUND GOOD!* This is a paradox that most people can prove through their own experience.

Musicians Who Care Too Much ...

Think of a time when you really needed to sound good. Maybe you were in school and you had to play for a "jury" (dig that word), or you were playing with musicians who were better than you and you really wanted to make an impression, or perhaps you were playing at a bar and all of a sudden a great musician walked in and sat down right in front of you! At that moment you wanted to play *so good!* How well did you play under those circumstances? Didn't your whole system freeze with the desire *to sound good?*

Now think back to times when it really didn't matter. You were playing with some buddies whom you trusted and who you know really liked you, or perhaps *you* were the most happening player in the group, and everyone was trying to impress you; or maybe it was 3:00 in the morning at a gig that no one had come to, and you had a few beers and couldn't have cared less. How did that sound? *You were grooving! Playing great and having a great time! You didn't care that much, and it really flowed.* Now what happened the next night? You thought about how good you had played the night before, *and you wanted to do it again!* How did this gig go? *NOT TOO GOOD!*

Usually, a bad gig follows a good gig for the following reason: you are thinking about how you made it happen the other night, and *you want to do it again.* That expectation causes the gig to go sour, and *you play lousy.* Or if you don't have a gig following that great experience, you can derive some comfort from your memory, and have a temporary feeling of high self-esteem. At insecure times in the day after a good gig, your mind can spin back to that special solo, and your calmness is restored. "Not to worry, I'M PLAYING GREAT, AREN'T I?" (And 24 hours later your mind has already exaggerated how good you really played!) But when the next gig finally arrives, there is no sense of letting the music develop the way it wants to that night, because you're looking for the same experience as the last time. The feeling is similar to taking a cruise on a sinking ship!

When I ask people in my clinics to contemplate this, 99% of them realize that they *played better when it didn't matter so much.* Think about it. What does that mean? When you *don't try as hard to be good, you play better.* It is a startling realization. Truly your own experience should prove to you that when you don't care, you play better. This is the opposite of what has always been thought of as true. *By not caring, you play better!*

An Involuntary Muscle

At this point in my clinics, I usually say, "Okay, now that we've proven that not caring leads to better playing, you're all never going to care again when you play, right?" That always gets some nervous laughter. Everyone knows that they won't be able to stop caring for even one second. Like an involuntary muscle, this concern just happens even as one approaches one's instrument. No matter how much people are intellectually aware, they will not be able to control their concern once they start to play. You may have read the most profound books on spiritual creativity and be certain that you know what it's all about, but when you approach the instrument, *that will not matter one bit. You will still be consumed with how good you sound!*

How many people are willing to get up on stage, play their instruments, and sound awful? And then, after sounding awful, how many people could say, "*I love myself?*" It may sound like "New Age philosophy," but if a true acceptance of oneself — if not actual love — is present, the *fear of failure will be gone!* "The easiest way to do art is to dispense with success and failure altogether and just get on with it," says Stephen Nachmanovich in his book, *Free Play.*[1] A person who is not afraid to die, knows how to live. A person who is not afraid to fail, succeeds. And a person who is not afraid to sound terrible may sound great. It isn't guaranteed, because there are other factors involved — but this essential element must be there.

Afraid of Sounding Bad ...

When you approach your instrument, no matter what lofty goals you say you have, wanting to sound good will predominate and render you impotent. For example, some horn players I've worked with didn't have a rich tone. In working with them, I've often found that they weren't really taking a deep breath and moving it through the horn. Doesn't it seem odd that horn players wouldn't take a deep breath? Why is that? Because *they are afraid to commit themselves to what's going to come out.* A really deep breath is going to add tone and weight to the next phrase, but the horn player is not sure about that next phrase. His lack of confidence causes a shorter breath, and a shorter breath

---

[1]Nachmanovich, Stephen. *Free Play*, Los Angeles: Jeremy P. Tarcher, Inc., 1990 (p.135)

creates a weaker tone, or a less rhythmic, or incomplete phrasing. The result confirms the player's fears. "Thought overheated loses its power ... Reason gives birth to doubt, which destroys the thought-power before it is able to fulfill its destiny."[2] If a horn player were to hold his breath as long as possible, almost passing out, and then release that breath into the horn while just moving his fingers over the keys, not worrying about the notes, he would experience a tone, force, dexterity and energy that he never knew existed. At that moment, the absolute necessity to exhale would override any trepidation about the musicality of the phrase.

Fear takes away the strength of what you are doing. Without fear of wrong notes, you would feel the body's craving for more air, and a new posture would emerge spontaneously. Pianists often show their fear in raised shoulders, stiff necks and tense minds. They don't let their arms move freely because they're *afraid to play poorly.* The result is anemic tone and rhythm. In this way their fears are manifested. In *Zen In The Art Of Archery*, the master admonishes his student, "The right shot at the right moment does not come because you do not let go of yourself. You do not wait for fulfillment, but brace yourself for failure."[3] These restrictive movements are the main cause of tendonitis and related physical ailments. It isn't piano playing that causes them. *Piano playing feels good to the muscles if you play freely.* I have had sore hands from carrying my luggage on tour or tightening a screw at home, (I don't claim mastery over those activities), but playing the piano *heals them!*

Once, while sitting in on a conducting class with Gunther Schuller, I noticed that a similar neurosis exists in the act of conducting. As the students in the class came up to conduct, their bodies would assume artificial postures. Their faces would reflect an austerity not relevant to the situation. I noticed that they showed a great concern for what they were doing, and this caused a stiffness in their whole persona. Some students would get up on their toes to emphasize the dynamics. Some would

---

[2]Hazrat Inayat Khan, *The Sufi Message* (p. 21)
[3]Eugen Herrigel, *Zen In The Art Of Archery* (p. 30)

lean awkwardly forward, and lose their center of gravity. Gunther would make comments to them about the extra effort they were making, and how it broke the fluidity of motion.

One chap, in Gunther's words, looked so sad, so sullen. Gunther invited him to enjoy the music. He kept replying that he was not sad, but concentrating. Even though I was only auditing this class, I almost yelled out, "Stop concentrating!"

I've only witnessed two conducting seminars — one with Gunther Schuller and the other with Pierre Boulez — and both stressed ease and simplicity of movement. Both conductors are famous for their simplicity, and it is a testimony to the power of self-assurance that these conductors can get more response from an orchestra with a subtle wave of a hand than others can with extraneous body-english and over-emphasis. What makes that happen? It is the drawing power of the inner self. It emerges when one has a true sense of oneself and one's powers.

From a technical point of view, conducting and piano playing are similar in that the rhythm must be entirely in the hand. Body-english is fine if it reflects joy or spirit, but if it is needed to make the hands work, it is detrimental. When Gunther got the students to relax the rest of their bodies, even a little bit, the crispness of the beat was somewhat lost because of their reliance on tension. I couldn't help thinking how easy conducting might be if one hadn't built up such a desire to conduct!

Why are you afraid to sound bad? Of course, it is understandable that on a gig you don't want to play badly because the leader may not want you back, and you will not put bread on the table. But don't you hate sounding bad when you're alone, or at a jam session, when there are no consequences? Don't you still feel that pressure to perform, even when it doesn't matter?

Isn't it true that when you sound bad, you feel bad? Don't you feel great the day after you sounded great? You walk around saying, "Wow, I am happening! I'm a happening guy! One of the cats!" But if you sound bad, you might walk around feeling, "I am nothing, less than nothing. Don't even talk to me, I don't deserve it." That may be exaggerating, but a lot of people can relate to these mood swings. The sad fact is that *most musicians judge their value as a person by their level of playing.* Therein lies an unhealthy linkage between musical proficiency and self-worth. It raises the stakes for what it means to play badly or well. This puts undue pressure on the act of playing — and as we just proved with the examples in our own lives, when the pressure is on to sound good we play worse — and so on and so forth.

Much of this mental/ spiritual/ physical /emotional struggle is experienced by even the greatest players. For sure, there are some who don't experience these problems; who take their music in stride, believing it to be only a part of who they are. Perhaps they have a sense of humor about it. But for most musicians, music students, and teachers, the musical life is pressure, even depression!

Does the following sound familiar? You think about your life all day long, your mind filled with issues. Should I move to New York? Should I stay in school? Should I become a teacher, or should I try and make it? If I got out of school, I could shed (practice) more, maybe get better. If you're a teacher, perhaps you feel the need to take a sabbatical so you can practice and become the player *your students think that you are!*

Music is not supposed to be a source of depression! Music is a gift. Music is ecstasy. Some people walk around wearing the badge proudly: "My whole life is music. I'm not a human being, I'm a musician. It isn't not necessary for me to interact with the 'squares,' I just care about playing" — and so on.

But, you have to discover a reason for living that *is more important than playing!* You need a sense of self that is stable, durable and not attached to your last solo. And, paradoxically, *that makes you play better!* It removes the consequences and puts everything in perspective. The pressure is gone ... and you play better.

As previously stated, it is extremely difficult, if not impossible, to just give up caring about how you sound, even if you know that that is ruining your performance. It takes more than knowing that intellectually in order to change. You may need a system of "reprogramming" to put your relationship to music on firmer ground.

Going Beyond

Music, unencumbered by unhealthy constraints, induces a state of ecstasy in the musician and audience. Music is there for our enjoyment and enrichment. Music is literally the sound of joy and devotion. It is a gift from God to allow us to express the incredible ecstasy of our inner nature. Falling short of that, music lays itself at our feet for expressing any of the countless feelings associated with the human condition. All other goals are limited goals. It's nice to play well, but that is not the point. My four-year-old daughter can walk over to the piano and enjoy herself more than ninety-five percent of the professional pianists. That's because *she has not defined herself as a pianist*.

Have you ever played an instrument other than your own, whether it be a saxophonist playing piano, or a pianist playing drums? Didn't you have a ball doing it? Playing the drums and thinking to yourself, "Yeah man, I'm cooking!" Bashing the cymbal, you feel like Elvin Jones, Philly Joe Jones, and Max Roach combined. You're having a great time, *and you sound terrible!* You were able to let go and feel benevolence towards your playing because *you don't call yourself a drummer!* You are free to have a good time.

Once you call yourself a drummer, it becomes more difficult to enjoy it unless you're a good player. You forget that it's more important to have a good time than to sound good.

There's nothing wrong with wanting to play well, but *needing* to play very well is the problem. The harder you try, the worse you play. Remember that your own experiences bear this out.

---

[4]Degas, Edgar. "Notebooks, 1856." In *Artists on Art*, edited by Robert Goldwater and Marco Treves. New York: Pantheon, 1945.

You Sounded Good, How Did I Sound?

"Only when he no longer knows what he is doing does the painter do good things."[4] So wrote Edgar Degas in 1856. The most mundane question in music is, *"How do I sound?"* Preoccupation with sounding good severely limits one's vision. If you asked most people why they play, they wouldn't say it was to sound good, but when you hear or watch them, you can tell that that becomes their overriding concern. In a relatively comfortable society like ours, musicians get caught up in mundane issues. You wake up in your little world and wonder how good you sound. Every ten minutes: "How do I sound? How do I sound now?" You walk around with that concern all day, and when you go to the gig, that's what you project.

Maybe you admit that your goal is to sound good, and you ask, What's wrong with that? Well, let's apply the issue to speaking. Imagine you asked someone, "What is your goal when you speak?" and they answered, "I just really want to *sound good! I really need to sound good, and I won't rest until I sound good!*" What would you think of that person? Probably that he's pretty shallow. But in music, people exert real effort, withholding love from themselves and others, *just trying to sound good*. What a foolish waste of a life!

When you have those good nights and you use the memory of them to feel secure, your sense of security is coming from outside you. That simply won't work for true fulfillment in your life. You don't need to play great. *You already are great.* Did you know that? If you play from that perspective, your music will become deeper. You will see beyond the limited goal of sounding good.

Chill Out

Did you know that it's not even important that you play another note of music again? In fact, many of you have a greater chance of happiness if you STOP PLAYING RIGHT NOW! UNLESS ... you change your relationship to playing and your relationship to yourself.

Playing can be a joyous celebration of who you are. When I play, I try to ignore the mundane considerations in my head and focus on the truth. I like to fill my head with words like "THANK YOU." Thank you for the experience of playing music. Thanks for this job in life. There are certainly many jobs that are less pleasant. Thanks for the fact that I'm in America, Denmark, France, or wherever, and not in a war-torn country! In fact, THANKS FOR THAT LAST BREATH I JUST TOOK!"

It's Only Music!

Here is a very simple test to prove that music is not that important:

Go to the kitchen and get a plastic bag. Place it over your head, tying the opening snugly around your neck so that no air can get through. Now, let's count to one hundred. By the count of twenty, let me ask you: how important is music? Are there any "burning issues"? Is Charlie Parker important? By the count of 35, would you be debating whether or not bebop was the real music? By 54, no doubt you would be contemplating whether music should swing, or whether free jazz really is where it's at. At 73, the question would burn in your consciousness; "Is Cecil Taylor for real?"

I think you get the point. The only thing that's really important is your next breath. We lose sight of reality very easily because of the little dictator in our heads: the mind. Our mind is always feeding us messages: "I must sound good;" "This is the right music, that is the wrong music;" "This is valid jazz, that is politically correct jazz" (yes, we have that these days). Or it sends us messages like: "I'm not supposed to play really great, because I'm a woman," or "I'm white," or "I'm European," or "only guys who live in New York can really play," or "I'm too old, and I can't learn to play any better." The mind is always supplying a steady stream of these illusions of limitation. They don't happen to be true, but they prevent you from seeing or hearing truth.

Music is the Icing on the Cake

The truth is that every breath is a gift, and *playing music is optional.* For the people in Somalia, food, not bebop, is important. For the people of Bosnia, it's peace. The absence of pain is important. Food, shelter, clean air, clean water, clothes to wear: these are more important than musical concerns, if not music itself. Music is not the cake. It's the icing on the cake. It is one of the enjoyments provided for us on this planet, in this life.

In the overall scheme of things, your level of proficiency is not important. Remember that you can benefit from realizing this, because if you decide it's not so important, *YOU MIGHT PLAY A LOT BETTER!*

In places like Bosnia and Somalia, music might very well be an important need for people to boost their spirits and give them courage. But music played under those circumstances tends to be the kind that matters, not the mundane kind that exists in the mind only. People without real problems can dwell too much in their thoughts. They may be consumed with their egotistical need to sound good. There is no ecstasy, love or spiritual sustenance.

Who Cares?

Who cares if you ever play another note of music? No one. What global purpose are you fulfilling? What burning need? Do you think that there is a shortage of good jazz musicians? My friends — FEAR NOT! There are holes in the ozone and the ozone layer is depleting. The seas are getting more polluted every year. There are fewer and fewer places where you can turn on the tap and drink the water. There are serious food shortages around the globe. But FEAR NOT, THERE IS A GLUT OF GOOD JAZZ MUSICIANS! A lot of them! Thousands come out of schools and universities every year. They multiply like coat hangers in your closet. Did you ever notice how you always have more and more coat hangers without ever buying one? Has anyone ever bought a coat hanger? So it is with competent, stylistically correct, "no voice of their own" type of jazz musicians. They can play fast. They can burn. They can play blues and rhythm changes. We get more of these people every year. So your participation is not important. We don't need you! Go back to your homes and start a new life!

Expression

What do we need? Even with all these well-trained improvisers, we don't have any more *artists* than we ever had. Artists take all that technology, all that language, and *say something*. They express something from very deep in their soul, or their deepest thoughts, political statements, love of homeland, love of self and of others, or just something that *needs to be said!* Maybe they're just having fun. Such people are not caught up in the petty issues of the day, but keep their eyes fixed on the truth as they know it. They may be visionaries, luminaries that light the way for the rest of us. They give us art from the soul, or the genitals, or from whatever drives them. When Ben Webster or Lester Young played a ballad, the atmosphere was super-charged. Their ballads were emotional, sexual or spiritual statements. Keith Jarrett says, "It is the individual voice, present to itself, that needs to be heard. We need to hear the process of a musician working on himself. We don't need to hear who is more clever with synthesizers. Our cleverness has created the world we live in, which in many ways we're sorry about."[5]

Jarrett's disdain for synthesizers aside, when many young players play a ballad, it becomes a chance to play more notes. Often they can't focus on a melodic statement and convey emotion, but are driven by myopic concerns, such as "burning." Young singers are often so preoccupied with their scat singing that they don't even check out the words to the song. They have the opportunity to tell us a story and make us feel its meaning, but they miss the point. Jarrett says, "We hear jazz musicians dabbling in world music and American Indian music, Minimalists

---

[5]Jarrett, Keith. New York Times article

filling as many sheets of paper as they can before they run out of 'idea,' industry reps dressed as players, players dressed as movie stars, indeed becoming movie stars———, black musicians without soul and countless 'studio' musicians reading newspapers in the control rooms (and getting paid handsomely for it, you might say being paid for their patience). We hear all this, but where is that voice, that original voice, that individual, primal need? Where is Miles? Where is the music?"[6]

Creativity and Discipline

It's nice to have the ability to burn and play on a million changes, but that is just the technology of the music, the language of improvisation. Bebop is a language, for example. If you strip away the romantic folklore about heroin, Harlem, and 52nd Street, it comes down to being a rhythmic and melodic language. If you relate to it as language, and not style, you can personalize it more easily. If you master that language, you can use it to say anything you want. In *The Music Of Santeria, Traditional Rhythms Of The Bata Drum*, the author says, "A study of New York (Bata) tradition reveals that while there are definitely correct and incorrect ways to play the salute rhythms, to a certain extent each generation, ensemble, and individual performer will internalize and recreate that tradition in his own musical voice."[7]

The goal of so many players is just to speak the language. Again, let's apply the issue to conversation. If you master the English language, does that make you a poet? Being able to speak in complete sentences is not an art, but a technical skill. Being a poet, a playwright or lyricist — that is art.

Looking at it this way resolves a long-standing controversy about technique versus creativity. One camp says, "I don't want to absorb too much technique, too much language, because it will squelch my creativity." Some people are afraid to learn too

---

[6]Ibid
[7]Amira, John & Cornelius, Steven. *The Music of Santeria, Traditional Rhythms of the Bata Drums*. Crown Point, IN: White Cliffs Media Company, 1992.

much for fear of losing their soul. But that doesn't hold up. What could the poet or playwright write without command of language? Composer Donald Erb says that if your talent can't stand a little training, it must have been pretty fragile to begin with.

The other camp states, "I play bebop well, therefore I am an artist." But that doesn't hold up either. Can you say, "I speak English well, therefore I am an artist"? Of course not. It all depends on what you say with language.

Helps the Planet

Music never dies in terrible times. To the contrary, it flourishes. At those times, the essence of what music can provide really comes through. The music that gives strength to deal with the atrocities of the day, a song that can articulate our pain, the dance that plays out our longing, the poetry that restores for us a moment of tranquility or incites us to riot — that's what becomes important.

Ultimately, musicians of the world must come to realize the potential of their calling. Like the shamans, we may serve as healers, metaphysicians, inciters, exciters, spiritual guides and sources of inspiration. If the musician is illumined from within, he becomes a lamp that lights other lamps. Then he is serving as a vehicle for the healing ocean of sound to wash over our planet and its people, healing what ails us. *Such music is truly important.* It is said that "only one who obeys can truly command." When the artist is immersed in service, giving himself up over and over again, another paradox occurs: *HE IS BEING SEEN BY ALL OTHERS AS A MASTER.*

Chapter 5
Fear-Based Playing

Fear, The Mind and The Ego

*For it is not death and pain that is a fearful thing,
but fear of death and pain*

Epictetus

Although music is commonly regarded as a gift from the gods, many suffer great pain and fear in attempting to play it. But this fear is quite irrational. Some of us play as if there were a gun being held to our head, and there usually is — because we're holding it! We assess our self-worth with every note, or with every stroke on the canvas; it doesn't matter which art form we are talking about. Enslaved by ego, we are encased in fear. What are the consequences of playing poorly? Nothing really, compared with the consequences of, say, jumping off a cliff. Yet if you ask some classical musicians to improvise, they might behave as if you were pushing them off a cliff!

Why is this so? As stated before, many of us have formed an unhealthy linkage between who we are and how we play. We fear being inadequate and that leads to ineffective playing, practicing, and listening. Fear closes all doors to the true self, that brilliant center where the ecstasy lies.

On the other hand, without excess mental baggage, playing music produces a feeling more exquisite than the sweetest nectar this world has to offer. It is the sound, smell and taste of grace. It may seem like a fairy tale, but this is the experience. However, the mechanism of fear makes such ecstasy unimaginable.

Stephen Nachmanovich, in his book, *Free Play*, writes of five fears that the Buddhists speak of that block our liberation: fear of loss of life; fear of loss of livelihood; fear of loss of reputation; fear of unusual states of mind; and fear of speaking before an assembly. He points out that fear of speaking before an assembly may seem light compared with the others, but we may take that to mean speaking up, or performing. Our fear of performing is "profoundly related to fear of foolishness, which has two parts: fear of being thought a fool (loss of reputation) and fear of actually being a fool (fear of unusual states of mind)."[1]

Then he says: "Let's add fear of ghosts."[2] I would take that to mean the implant of fear by authority figures no longer present in our lives, but the echo of whose voice remains to control us (teachers, parents and so forth). Or it could literally be ghosts; the legacy of music left by the great masters. So many musicians are filled with too much awe for that legacy and never feel "worthy" of adding to it.

People who have unusual difficulty learning and playing might have been told at an early age that playing music is very difficult, or that they were untalented. Once that is believed, it becomes very hard to progress. The menacing voices from childhood become the voices in one's own head: "You're no good, stupid!" The messages can be more subtle than that, but lingering fear of being a fool translates into fear of not being worthy, of not having value. I see that in so many students. The drive to assuage those fears derails the quest for mastery.

Where does fear originate? From the mind? Yes, but not the "universal mind," or the "over mind," or the "collective unconscious." Rather, fear originates in our "little mind." One may call that little mind the ego. Let us set aside the Freudian and post-Freudian debate on what the ego is or isn't. For our purposes, we are referring to the ego as the limited "I" consciousness. It is the lens through which we perceive our

---

[1]Nachmanovich, Stephen. *Free Play*, Los Angeles: Jeremy P. Tarcher, Inc., 1990. (p. 135)
[2]Ibid (p. 135)

separateness from each other. Separateness invites comparison and competition. This is where problems orginate: he's younger than I, more talented, and so forth.

By contrast, dissolution of the ego and union with the divine is the goal of Indian music. Oneness with the universal mind is "called *sadhana*, the supreme act of ego surrender of merging individual identity into the object worshiped."[3] The trance-dancer has the same goal.

Tyrannized by our egos, we live in a state the Hindus call *maya*, or delusion. Engrossed in *maya*, we can't see the magnificence of who we really are. We think we need so much. Desires multiply, and we know nothing of real inner happiness. "The clouds of emotion obscure the clear sight of the soul."[4] We seek safety in "job security" and obsess about our level of play. Fear sabotages us at every turn.

Taking an honest inventory of our musicianship is difficult. Some feel more comfortable condemning themselves totally than accurately assessing their strengths and weaknesses. They are usually defeated by a sense of futility before they play the first note. Others believe themselves to be better than they are, not wanting to face the gaps they need to work on. Their performances tend to hit or miss, but they rationalize that their best performances are how they really play, and their worst performances are flukes. *It's not really them.* In this way they avoid fixing and cleaning up what needs to be fixed and cleaned. In either case, the disclosure of flaws in their playing hurts. Because there is so much emotion attached to the flaws, the latter group would try to overlook them, and the former would use them as evidence that they stink. Improvement is delayed for years, or perhaps forever.

---

[3]Holroyde, Peggy. *The Music of India.* New York: Praeger Publishers, Inc., 1972. (p. 45)
[4]Hazrat Inayat Khan, *The Sufi Message* (p. 19)

Fear Based Playing

You start a nice and tasty solo and a little voice goes off in your head, *"It isn't good enough! I have to play hipper. This should burn more. It has to be more complex ..."* or some thought like that. Whatever comes easily isn't good enough because, in your mind, *you're* not good enough! You start thumping your feet, trying to coerce music out of yourself, or sing along for emphasis. You are straining or "digging in," and at that moment, the solo loses all subtlety and groove. It sounds nervous, and the tone is lost. Perhaps you start rushing or over-playing and just then you might get lost in the form or in the time. Then, fear of looking foolish causes you to sit there stiffly and *pretend you're not lost!* Sound familiar?

Fear of inadequacy causes you to ignore the ideas that want to come naturally. They seem too obvious or "not hip enough." But they are, in fact, the right stuff. Trapped in thought, you cannot groove. "As soon as we reflect, deliberate, and conceptualize, the original unconscious is lost and a thought interferes."[5]

Remember that fear of sounding bad robs the music of all its strength. Believing that playing is a difficult, painful process, we shun anything that seems easy.

Here is another example of fear sabotaging your playing: Let's say you have been practicing something for a while, and you have a great desire to hear yourself play it in performance; in fact, you feel *pressured* to play it. Why? Because you want to convince yourself that your practicing wasn't a waste of time. So ready or not, you *will* play it! You'll get it in there somehow. But like a cake that hasn't been fully baked, it comes out raw. You have fallen into an ego trap and sound terrible. Had the piece you were practicing been fully absorbed, it would have come out naturally and enhanced your performance. But if you had to think about it, it wasn't "ready to serve." Your sight was clouded by ego in this case. Fear of wasting your time (fear of

---

[5]Eugen Herrigel, *Zen In The Art Of Archery* (p. viii)

loss of life, perhaps?) caused you to rush material into your performance before it was ready. You might have very well given up practicing that item, either because you thought you had it, or because you were completely fed up waiting for it to work.

In your delusion, you think that you must know eighty-five styles of music. But the fact is that I've never heard any player of note who plays in any style but his own. Have you? It may not be an original style, but it is the style he has embraced. You may think that you can never repeat yourself, but jazz is not total improvisation. If you listen to any great improviser, from Art Tatum to Charlie Parker to John Coltrane, you'll notice that they *always repeat themselves.* Transcribe their solos and you'll find that they are always playing the same lines. Sometimes they are even playing the same things in the same places. The improvisational aspect is the juxtaposition of those phrases, but the notes within the phrases are often the same. As they are not afraid of doing this, it comes out as "their voice" rather than sounding repetitive. Don't be afraid to play the phrases you know. Those are the ones that groove. Conversely, all the great improvisers say that when you take a chance, leave fear behind and go with the flow, so to speak; you'll usually land on your feet. Fear either doesn't allow you to take a chance, or if you do, it makes you falter. I am not a skier, but I imagine that when Olympic skiers make those huge jumps, they'd better not flinch, or else we might see two upside-down feet with skis on them sticking up out of the snow!

Fear of ghosts is so common in young players. If you're a pianist, for example, you wouldn't want to be thinking about Art Tatum before you play! That would be like shooting yourself in the foot. If you want to be funky and rhythmic, thinking of Herbie Hancock would inhibit that. While playing, say the words "Keith Jarrett" in your mind and see how much fun *that* is. Listening to a Miles Davis quintet album from the sixties before you go to the gig could be a disaster. Overcome by the need to be "modern" and "complex," you might just end up sounding terrible. At those moments your shoulders go up, your neck strains, your face crumples up into a prune as you try to be somebody else.

You deny your birthright to create, and are condemned to recreate! Most of us would settle for being able to recreate these musicians, but since most of us are not on that level of proficiency, we probably could never do it convincingly and would overextend ourselves trying. Even if you successfully recreate someone else's sound, you may lack power and depth, since you are fearful of over-stepping the bounds of that style (and thus appearing foolish).

Miles Davis came into Charlie Parker's band following Dizzy Gillespie. If you listen to those early recordings, Miles sounds as if he were struggling a bit. With the force of Gillespie still ringing in his ears, he had not yet found his center of power. It was only later, when Miles found his own approach, that his voice, tempo, style, power and grace emerged.

Without "fear of ghosts," you might make music of real depth. Without fear of sounding bad, you are free to be real. Fear lurks in the mind. If you want to be free, master your mind. "You will be free of the world's turbulence as soon as you calm your thoughts."[6]

Bobby McFerrin said in a workshop that "improvisation is the courage to move from one note to the next." It's that simple. Once you conquer that basic fear, when you are able to make that leap from one note to the next without thinking or preparing for it, then you are improvising.[7]

When you move from one note to the next, the audience will hear you whether they understand jazz or not, and they'll want to hear you again. But, fear won't let you do that. Ego makes you lose sight of the whole, and fixate instead on "hipness," which narrows the interest of the music to you and perhaps a few fellow students. And those fellow students sit there biting their nails and actually hoping you *don't sound good!* (I'll expound on this later).

---

[6]Millman, Dan. *Way Of The Peaceful Warrior, A Book That Changes Lives.* Tibouron California: HJ Kramer, Inc., 1984. (p. 81)
[7]Milkowski, Bill. "Swing, Soul, Sincerity— A Bobby Mcferrin Workshop". *DownBeat*

Don't make the mistake of thinking that the audience's ears don't matter. On the contrary. They are more objective in what they hear than the musician. A fearless improviser who likes to turn himself on in public will have an impact on any audience. Bill Evans was quite eloquent on this subject when he said, "I do not agree that the layman's opinion is less of a valid judgment of music than that of the professional musician. In fact, I would often rely more on the judgment of the sensitive layman than that of a professional, since a professional, because of his constant involvement with the mechanics of music, must fight to preserve the naivete that the layman already possesses."[8] "Mechanical" concerns obscure "naivete."

Just before I play, I like to feel that no one has ever played the piano before, that I'm in complete virgin territory, and that *every note I play is the most beautiful sound I've ever heard.*

In fear, we expect; with love, we accept.

---

[8] Bill Evans from his video, *The Universal Mind of Bill Evans: The Creative Process and Self Teaching.* Rhapsody Films Inc.

Chapter 6

Fear-Based Practicing

*The wise man in the storm prays to God, not for
safety from danger, but for deliverance from fear.*

Ralph Waldo Emerson

*J*ust as fear pollutes the environment for creativity, it also
inhibits effective study. The mind wreaks havoc, and the ego
has a picnic. For example, you want to be a great jazz player,
and your mind tells you that you must succeed by a certain age.
If you're 18, you must succeed by 21. When that doesn't happen,
you give yourself until 25. By 25, it's 30 ... and so on. And if
you're 35, it's 40, and by 40 you feel that "the parade has passed
you by."

Your mind might be driven by the thought that you must be
an expert in all styles of music; therefore, you have a great deal
of material that must be covered. You feel as though there is a
huge workload ahead of you with so little time. You experience a
fear of dying before you'll get it all together!

You see, fear has ruined your practicing by *rushing you
through the material,* rendering you unable to absorb anything.
You try to cover too much ground every time you practice, barely
skimming the surface of each item, and then moving on. You
ignore the fact that you can barely execute the material, because
you have no time to notice that. After all, *there's so much to
practice and so little time!* It's frustrating — even though you're
practicing all this stuff, your playing is not improving much.
Nothing is mastered. Hearing yourself play the exercise correctly
once or twice, you rationalize that you have it. The only problem
is if you come back to it ten minutes later, you find that you

don't have it! You are practicing many things, but nothing is sinking in, and nothing you practice is surfacing when you play. You never stop to think that you should be playing better for all this practice. You have a belief system, rooted in fear, that *you're not supposed to play that well anyway!* The results you're getting are confirming that belief.

While moving quickly through material, you're under the delusion that you are making progress. Spending enough time learning something would feel interminably slow, but that is the way of true growth. It takes what it takes. The fact is that if you don't stay with the material long enough for it to become comfortable, you'll find that it doesn't stay with you. *Then you will truly be wasting your time! It really doesn't pay to move on until something is mastered.*

A fearful mind won't allow you to concentrate and absorb. Even while focusing on one thing, the mind is exerting subtle or not-so-subtle pressure with the thought of the other things that need tending to. This creates a very anxious and insecure feeling. When you skim the surface, you acquire many bad habits with regard to tempo, fingering and other details. Repetition of these bad habits causes them to grow ingrained ever more deeply into your subconscious, so that you are actually doing what I call *negative practice.* In this way, one hour of practicing is better than two, thirty minutes is better than an hour, and *no practicing at all would be preferable to that kind of negative practice!*

Many musicians are so fixated on complex elements that they fail to spend enough time on the basics. As a result, they tend to have all sorts of glitches — basic gaps in their playing. For example, if basic chord progressions are not fully digested, you will struggle with most standard tunes. Eighty percent of all jazz standards are comprised of the II-V-I progression, a succession of chords. If you really master that progression in all keys, you'll find that you can fly through most tunes instantly. But before mastering this fundamental progression, your restless mind may have already driven you to study more exotic ones. By not having properly learned II-V-I, you are probably doomed to fail in the playing of more modern progressions as well as in the basic ones. Your fear in this case might be a fear of dying before you are considered "modern."

Why do most of us move on when we haven't yet mastered anything? *We are afraid that we won't become great players, and that becomes a self-fulfilling prophecy.*

You move on because you think there isn't enough time to learn all the things you need in order to become a great player. You move on, leaving the previous material in an unusable state. *And you never become a great player.* Your mind has played a trick on you.

Dysfunctional practicing is one by-product of fear and ego. Sometimes the mind is so restless and filled with anxiety that you can't practice at all. A person in this state thinks himself uncommitted or just "lazy" because he can never get it together to practice. If this is you, be kind to yourself. You're not lazy, you're just *completely overwhelmed!* In your mind, there is so much to accomplish that you can't get started. You're caught in an energy field of angst.

Does the following sound familiar? You wake up, look at your list of things to practice and say, "I need a cup of coffee before I get started." So you drink your coffee and decide to read the paper as well. There's no better time to read the paper than with that first cup of coffee (and, of course, we all know how genuinely concerned you are about current events). The time slips away, and you look at your list, then your watch, and say to yourself, "Well, I don't have time for that right now. Maybe after lunch." After lunch, you think about that list and decide, "Maybe I'll just make some phone calls first and then I'll get right down to it." After the phone calls, you head for your instrument, and as you do, you pass the kitchen and think, "Maybe just one more cup of coffee. After that I'll be pumped up from the caffeine and I'll burn through that list!" You drink the coffee, come bounding out of the kitchen, look at the list and exclaim, "One more phone call!" The phone call was frustrating, and you're too wound up to practice. Now you need to cool out.

Looking at the list again, you think, "I'm a little too tired to practice right now. I think I'll watch some television for half an hour, then I'll be ready to go." You watch TWO HOURS of television and say, "Oh, I'm too spaced out to do anything now. I'll wait until after dinner." After dinner you yawn and say, "That was a good dinner. I need to digest for a while." Or you go out partying so that you can forget the failures of the day. You procrastinated the whole day away. Perhaps some drug is part of the diversion. You might think that after a nice joint you'll really be able to get into it. Four or five minutes feel great, but soon you're too spaced out (or hungry again) to concentrate on a process, and it's time to tune out. Real practicing never takes place, and you go to bed disappointed in yourself again. This feeds the fire of self-loathing. You try to ease the pain with a silent promise to "wake up earlier tomorrow" and get started right away. It is your overactive mind that cannot concentrate — maybe if you wake up an hour earlier, you might accomplish something before your mind wakes up! But, alas, as you open your eyes, your mind is staring you in the face, smiling and saying, "Good morning, sleepy-head. I thought you'd never wake up!" Your mind is right there waiting for you again, and that day slips away like all the others. Instead of moving forward a tiny bit each day and evolving, you spend most of the day in your head obsessing about your life. I joke with students in my clinics, saying that I want them to borrow five minutes from those hours they spend each day obsessing about themselves, and use that time to practice!

Why does one do nothing when one cares so passionately about playing music? It is *not* laziness; it *is* a sense of being overwhelmed. You need to know this. It's like the alcoholic acknowledging, "I'm not a bad person, I'm a sick person." It allows one to feel a bit more self-compassion.

If your expectations can't be met, lowering them is in order. For example, don't think that you must practice three to five hours every day. Who's got three to five hours? You don't realize the benefits of focused, patient practice for even five minutes! Five-minute interludes center the mind. Many people feel the onset of anxiety (another word for fear) at the mere thought of practice. Their anxiety is caused by two quandaries: how long should they practice, and what should they begin with. These people are trapped in their heads. If you fit one or more of the profiles I've just described, I hope that you will find answers later in this book as to how to change your mental landscape and begin to move forward.

Being afflicted by the inability to act, you feel locked out of a glass-enclosed world of functioning musicians. You bang on the glass with scattered practice habits, but nobody hears you. All your attempts to enter are futile. Fear of not becoming great has kept you from becoming great. To find a way out of this dilemma, a thorough re-programming of your mind is necessary.

Chapter 7
Teaching Dysfunctions:
Fear-Based Teaching

It is not death that a man should fear, but he should fear never beginning to live.

$\mathcal{N}$achmanovich makes a great statement: "To *educe* means to draw out or evoke that which is latent: education then means drawing out the person's latent capacities for understanding and living, not stuffing a (passive) person full of preconceived knowledge."[1] Therein lies the reason why so many are overwhelmed, as described in the previous chapter. They're very likely to be "stuffed with preconceived knowledge" rather than having had their "latent capabilities" drawn out.

This is an important point. It is common practice to give weekly assignments rather than *support the student in understanding the material.* I firmly believe that educators should rethink this approach. Burying the student in assignments will often sink him. Sometimes it is necessary to discontinue lessons until the student regains his bearings. But since many were taught this way, as a result, they teach this way. Fear and anxiety are passed on from generation to generation. Also there are those who occupy positions of authority, but are incompetent — and that too causes fear.

The world is blessed with many accomplished, even inspired, teachers, but there are also many teachers that fit the description above. Too many.

---

[1] Nachmanovich, Stephen. *Free Play*, Los Angeles: Jeremy P. Tarcher, Inc., 1990. (p. 118)

Such a teacher may put emphasis on the wrong things. Perhaps he cannot impart the right information that would solve the students' dilemmas, having never solved them himself. The student knows something is wrong, but may not realize that his teacher is also in the dark.

I want to reiterate that there are many great and effective teachers. However, I am not referring to them at the moment. The reason I am talking about poor teachers is that we need to articulate all barriers to mastery and, if possible, to restore clarity.

A frustrated teacher has a self-loathing problem that grows over time. He might appear to be generally disgruntled. He is conspicuously absent from important musical events, such as when a great player comes to town. Sometimes a student comes along who plays well and forces the teacher to confront his own ego. The teacher has to find ways to guide the student, while secretly he may fear or resent that student for his or her gifts.

Such gifted students are only temporarily handicapped. They usually go on and find their way. But for borderline players, the quality of the teacher may mean the difference between becoming a musician and not. Some don't make it — and *many become teachers themselves!* Years go by while they slip further into denial.

More often I find teachers who are good players, but stumped as to how to get better. They've reached a plateau that they can't surpass. Secretly, they suffer all the same frustrations of the students they are counseling. Often during clinics, one or more of the teachers attending will come up to me discreetly and whisper, "You know, you just told my story." We'll hang out for a while, and I'll listen to his or her plight, trying to recommend a course of action. Sometimes they are humble and honest enough to admit their frailties to their students, and express a willingness to figure it out together. It becomes a mutual journey. I really like seeing that.

Teachers who need to change are in the same situation as their pupils. The student complains that he cannot reprogram himself because he is so busy *going to school,* and the teacher has the same lament because he is so busy *teaching school!* There is a way for anyone to change their tendencies, level of proficiency, and, in fact, their life with steady, conscious action. But without such a plan, these musicians grow progressively unhappier as time passes, because they are living a lie. It becomes more painful to carry the burden as the years go by.

But you *can* change with self-effort. Get honest, and get control of your mind.

Chapter 8
Hearing Dysfunctions:
Fear-Based Listening

Joyous we too launch out on trackless seas,
Fearless of unknown shores.

Walt Whitman

*J*azz students with ego problems actually fear hearing good music. I was once in a town performing with a great group. The next day I did a clinic at the local music school for about thirty people. I asked how many students had attended the concert the night before. Only three people raised their hands. This was not New York or a town where one could hear this quality of music very often. I was shocked. I told them that if a gig or other important commitment didn't keep them from attending, they might want to reevaluate their motives for studying music — because if this was what they really wanted to do in life, why would they miss an opportunity to hear how beautiful it can be? Hearing inspired performers invigorates us and reinforces our commitment. However, if one is merely stroking oneself, one would avoid awareness of great players. Musicians like these prefer the comfort and safety of their hobbit holes!

Who wants to admit that he hates to hear a great player? But some find it too painful. It fuels the fires of their self-loathing: "If he plays great, then I am worthless," is how it goes. I know that this applies to many of you.

I experienced the transition between fear-based listening and listening with love when, as mentioned earlier, I was listening to Horowitz with my teacher in Brazil. I suddenly noticed how twisted and tense my body was. Being released from my ego at that moment allowed me to experience the joy in his playing.

You should listen the same way that you play, practice or teach: with love and openness. In this way, you become absorbed in the moment and lose yourself in the music. You may find that your playing has changed through osmosis. This point has been proven to me many times. There is a radio station in New York City that celebrates the birthdays of various musicians by playing their music all day, or sometimes all week. One time they were playing Art Blakey for several days. I had the radio on that station all weekend. Day and night, listening or not, Art Blakey was drifting through my ears. Sometimes I would sit and listen, other times I would be busy. It occurred to me that I had never listened to so much continuous Blakey before. Monday night, on my way to the Village Vanguard for my regular gig with the Mel Lewis Orchestra, I was still listening to him on the car radio.

When we started to play, I noticed that everything felt different. I had automatically absorbed Blakey's groove, and I was playing things with a different gait. Others in the band acknowledged the change in feeling. Effortless listening is like breathing. It nourishes you without your even knowing it.

Another time, while teaching at the Schweitzer Institute in Sandpoint, Idaho, I had the opportunity to listen to more orchestral and chamber music than I've ever listened to in a small period of time. One night I played solo piano and improvised like never before. It was as if a spontaneous orchestra piece were "channeling" through me. Weeks of inhaling all that great music were now manifesting in my playing.

You even have to remain open to music that doesn't at first grab you. If you do not have a passion for certain styles of music, it's good to be honest about that. But as a student of music, it is also good to try to expand your limits. All music is related. Different types of music offer lessons to enrich you. What blocks listening is the same element that blocks playing: mental noise.

Years ago, when I would see a sky filled with stars, my mind would say, "Wow, I *should* really dig this sky." I was actually pressuring myself to love the sky. Later, as my mind became quieter, I could stand out there and merge with the beauty. The same is true of music. Don't try to listen, but just *let yourself listen*. As you "merge with the beauty," you become uplifted; and if you listen deeply, you hear things.

Once, while listening to music all night, I heard an absolute relationship between Joni Mitchell, Bela Bartok, and South Indian music. It was a revelation to me – but was it not there before? These insights were caused by my immersion in the music.

The Sufi Master, Hazrat Inayat Khan, says: "There are different ways of listening to music. There is a technical state when a person who is developed in technique and has learned to appreciate better music, feels disturbed by a lower grade of music. But there is a spiritual way, which has nothing to do with technique. It is simply to tune oneself to the music; therefore the spiritual does not worry about the grade of the music. No doubt, the better the music the more helpful it is to a spiritual person; but at the same time one must not forget there are lamas in Tibet who do their concentrations and meditations while moving a kind of rattle, the sound of which is not especially melodious. They cultivate thereby that sense which raises a person by the help of vibration to the higher planes. There is nothing better than music as a means for the upliftment of the soul."[1]

It is egoless listening that tunes you to the music. The same quality of listening applies when playing with a group. Fear-based listening is *trying* to play with others while being preoccupied with yourself. One of my students said that his self-consciousness got in the way of listening to others while he was playing. He found himself listening and *trying to respond*. That's partially right. You want to listen and respond, but you can't plan your response or you'll lose the moment: that precious

---

[1]Hazrat Inayat Khan, *The Sufi Message*.

connection with true self. This same person said that once, when he was playing with a group, he kept repeating to himself like a mantra, "Don't think, listen ... Don't think, listen ..." He realized that he was so busy saying, "Don't think, listen," that he wasn't listening. That is called *trying not to try* and it is one of the follies of an intrusive mind. In the book, *The Music Of Santeria, Traditional Rhythms Of The Bata Drums*, by John Amira and Steven Cornelius, the authors point out the nature of listening: "In the early stages of learning it is not uncommon to lose track of the very sounds that one creates on his own drum amongst the broader sounds of the ensemble. While disconcerting at first, this may also be a positive sign, for it suggests that one's ears are experiencing and assimilating the totality of the ensemble rather than being locked onto a single musical line."[2]

We need this awareness to attain oneness with the music, and with ourselves. There's a nectar that flows from the fruit of egolessness; it is the bliss that we have sought all our lives.

---

[2]*The Music Of Santeria, Traditional Rhythms Of The Bata Drums*, by John Amira & Steven Cornelius.

Chapter 9
Fear-Based Composing

$\mathcal{F}$ear of composing, like fear of playing, is irrational. The source is the same: fear of writing bad compositions. There is really no importance to writing a good composition other than to nourish your feeling of self-worth. If one weren't in need of validation as a composer, one could delightfully doodle, happily filling many music notebooks. If a person has acquired the tools of composing through study, then that expertise will manifest in his compositions. It must be said again and again: *without the need for self-validation, talent and acquired knowledge flow naturally.*

Random Composition

"Channeling" composition involves the same process as improvisation — *through the grateful acceptance of whatever comes out.* I call this random composition: Filling a piece of paper with random notes.

The most anxious moment for a composer is staring at a blank piece of paper. It is much easier to edit material than it is to create from nothing. Putting notes on paper without attachment is a great start!

Once you have created "some stuff," you can begin to edit. Through the process of variation, you can create more music or improve upon what you've got. However, any sense of attachment to the work prevents you from seeing the possibilities. For example, whatever notes you write can be developed by varying the order, the octave, the transposition, and so on. If you do this *without any emotional attachment,* without the need to create anything *worthwhile* (the same old trap), you are likely to come up with more attractive sets of notes. Putting some of them together, you can create longer ideas from the embryo of your original random choices.

Other elements can be varied as well. For example, you can harmonize a melody, then get rid of the melody and write a new one to the harmony. Then you can re-harmonize that melody, and you have created two melodies and two sets of changes from the embryo. Now you can modify those progressions and melodies in many other ways. Bob Brookmeyer talks about polishing the music: you polish and polish through variation, until it shines with continuity. But I would add that you must resist as long as possible the temptation to make "a piece" out of it. Just keep doodling. The longer you resist identifying the piece, the more "stuff happens." As you detach, the piece seems to "write itself." And this is very important: *you must feel free to throw things away!* Entering into greater detail would be the subject of another book — but what is important is the principle of *composing with detachment.*

I was recently working on several pieces for large ensembles. Using a computer, I had the benefit of copying, erasing, or re-working the ideas instantly. The result was that I could stretch the ideas any way that I wanted to. People commented that I must have learned a lot about computers from this experience, but I learned much more about composition. I would rework and rework the piece until it changed into something that I wasn't expecting at all. Another benefit was that *so much music emerged*, like having a pipeline to a never-ending ocean of ideas. It is important to note that sometimes, when I couldn't hear anything at all and felt no inspiration, writing random notes and playing with them would cause the creative juices to flow.

Nothing is so inhibiting as *needing to write something brilliant.* Once a good friend of mine was writing an opera and really experiencing a block. He was duly tormented, believing that "composing is a painful process." He talked wistfully about a certain opera as being considered "the greatest opera since World War Two." I told him, "It sounds to me like you are trying to write the greatest opera since Desert Storm! I have an idea. Why don't you just write a bad opera? That should be easy." My friend laughed uncomfortably with me, but I could sympathize with his dilemma. You always want to do well, but the recurring paradox is that you have a much better chance of doing well if you let go of the anxiety and just get on with it.

Try writing three bad pieces a day. I bet you can't do it. Your talent will sabotage you and cause some great music to come out! Another composer-friend of mine told me, "Kenny, I know that that just doesn't work. I've written a ton of bad pieces over the last thirty years, and it hasn't done anything for me." I said to him, "Ah yes, but did you ever *try to write a bad piece?* That is the liberation that I'm talking about!"

You may think that this stuff sounds great, and that reading about it has the power to change your life. But I guarantee that the next time you play or compose, *you'll act as if you've heard and read nothing!* As I said before, trying to sound good is a reflex. The ego is like an involuntary muscle. You wish you weren't so self-absorbed, but you just can't help it. And your self-absorption doesn't necessarily manifest itself in most obvious ways. For example, you may think you're humble because you put yourself down all the time, but you're still caught up in ego because you have to be self-centered in the extreme to feel that bad about yourself!

The taming of the mind, the dissolution of the ego and the letting go of all fears can only evolve through *patient practice.* There is nothing worth attaining on this or any other planet that doesn't take practice. As you do this, you become aware of another "space."

Chapter 10
"The Space"

Making The Connection

"You must be nothing but an ear that hears what the universe of the world is constantly saying within you."

Rabbi Dov Baer of Mezritch

There is a place inside each of us where perfection exists. The genius, God, lives there. All the creative possibilities of the universe are to be found there. It is the innate ability of each of us to be God, to behave with extreme dignity, to conduct our business in a righteous manner, and to channel an endless stream of life-enhancing ideas and celebratory sounds for the upliftment of mankind. This joyful noise is the sound of the Supreme Being manifesting through us. If we surrender our desires, we will hear it. At first it will seem distant, like the sound of the ocean when you put an ear to a conch shell, but with practice, one can hear the divine "unstruck sound" and become enveloped by it. The outer music is then imbued with the light of the universe and its great transforming power. A most worthy goal is to live one's life and perform all of one's duties from this inner space. "Out of the fullness of this presence of mind, disturbed by no ulterior motive, the artist who is released from all attachment must practice his art."[1]

From this space, there is great compassion, and great love, as well as great detachment. A person becomes the supreme

---

[1]Eugen Herrigel, *Zen In The Art Of Archery* p. 38

enjoyer, observer, and doer. His involvement in life is total. He fully participates in the world, yet is not ensnared by it. There is no fear, because he is not attached to the results of actions. Practice takes no patience, since there is no burning need to reach a goal. There is simply the celebration of the doing, the learning, the achieving and enjoying. To be sure, he experiences the entire range of emotions, but he is not attached. Therefore, he can live his life and make his moves in harmony with his inner self and the outer universe. He frequently receives intuition about what to do next, and he follows it fearlessly. Paradoxically, detachment causes his actions to have great purpose and result in great success. The abundance of the universe tends to rain on such a person; however, if it does not, that too is all right.

In terms of a musical life, this translates into fearless expression: just moving from one note to the other, seeking unity with one's own inner self, and unlocking an ocean of music for others to replenish their spirits. The entire process of learning becomes a joyful game, because the student is not attached to results but observes himself with one-pointed focus.

"If vibratory activity is properly controlled, man may experience all of life's joy, and at the same time not be enslaved by it."— *"in the control abides the whole of what is called mastership."*[2]

Detachment is an essential quality for one to become established in that space. Expectations create agitation in the mind, and then merging with one's self is not possible. The great Siddha Yoga master, Swami Chidvilasananda has said, "Expectation exists when there is fear."[3] The fear of not getting what we want is predominant in Western society, but the never-ending quest to satisfy "needs" masks our deepest desire: oneness with the divine force. The ego refracts the pure light of One and creates the illusion of many, and we seek union in the pursuit of

---

[2]Hazrat Inayat Khan, *The Sufi Message*, p. 20
[3]Darshan Magazine, March 1994, p. 42

externals. We think that if we have enough of what we want, we will be safe. But from the inner space, one realizes that everything one needs and desires already exists within. Christ, or Jesus said, "First seek ye the Kingdom of God and all else will be added." He also said, "The Kingdom of Heaven lies within." I take those statements to mean that our true fulfillment is to be found in the Kingdom, and that Kingdom lies within ourselves.

The Inner Space is the place where joy, pleasure and fulfillment – worldly and otherwise – are available in unlimited supply. Acceptance of these gifts allows the flow to increase. Performances given from this state are said to be greatly inspired, leaving their audiences profoundly moved. A concert given by a performer who has attained this state is regarded as an event not to be missed.

As musicians, we have the potential of doing great things. Everyone can remember at least one great concert they've been to. The performance was so inspired that it stayed with the audience well after they went home. Perhaps the fragrance of it was still there the next day. The feeling it created caused those present to behave differently for a while, possibly with more grace, with more mindfulness of the soul. Spiraling to deeper levels of consciousness, the performer takes us beneath the layers of illusion and peels us like an onion. He gives us the spiritual nourishment that we so deeply need.

A true master is not just a master of technique or language, but of himself. He can sit serenely in the center of that space while performing his actions to perfection. This is a state of selflessness and absolute concentration is called *samadhi* by Hindus and Buddhists. Meditation is the tool most often used to achieve this state. Once *samadhi* is achieved, *one may perform all actions in that state.* In a conversation I had with Toots Thielemans on the subject, he referred to it as "ground level zero."

Mildred Chase, in her wonderful book, *Just Being At The Piano,* expressed it beautifully: "I am now able to reach a state of being at the piano from which I come away renewed and at peace with myself, having established a harmony of the mind, heart, and body."[4]

A quiet mind allows the artist to tap into the wellspring of Divine Music within. Having experienced that state, all other goals seem insignificant.

When you do the meditations in this book, notice if you feel a quieting of the mind and/or a feeling of expansiveness. It is from there that we must learn to play. The goal is to get beyond the mind, that noisy little stream of thoughts, and merge into the ocean of consciousness. From there, you experience an *absence of things* — an absence of effort, of caring, the absence of desire or of needs. Things become quite simple.

If you have experienced this space even for a moment, you become determined to get there again. You're amazed that you've spent so much of your life tyrannized by your mind when this "space" existed. (Wow – I can actually feel like this without cognac?). In the inner space there are no conditions, no requirements; you just are. You are making conscious contact, forming an informational highway, with the higher, or inner self. This is the spiritual connection that many artists speak of as the primary force in their art. When one is motivated by a deeper sense of purpose than just making "good music," one reaches greater heights.

"In music and dance we soon become very aware
of this world alive with gods and goddesses."[5]

Gunther Schuller told me that after his wife Marjorie died, he couldn't write music for almost a year. Then one day, it burst forth from him in a tidal wave of emotion. He wrote a great

---

[4]Chase, Mildred. *Just Being at the Piano.* Berkeley: Creative Arts Books.
[5]Holroyde, Peggy. *The Music of India.* New York: Praeger Publishers, Inc., 1972 (p. 49).

piece for her in four days. Motivated not by twelve-tone correctness, the music scene in general or "history," he wrote what had to be written. All of his expertise was now in the service of his need to express. Mr. Schuller won a Pulitzer Prize for this piece. He told me that he had entered pieces many other times and had never won. But that piece, a catharsis for him, was the one that most impressed the panel of judges.

Tapping this source is not necessarily spiritual in a religious way. The mind is thought to be divided into three parts: the conscious, subconscious, and super-conscious. If you lean towards that view, you might refer to the space as the super-conscious mind. As an artist, one would want to transcend the conscious mind, where all the noise resides, change the negative messages that have been stored in the subconscious mind and become attuned to the super-conscious mind. That is where inner perfection may exist. Changing the messages in the subconscious is a matter of steady self-effort and patient reprogramming.

Bill Evans calls this space the universal mind. "I believe that all people are in possession of what might be called a universal mind. Any true music speaks with this universal mind to the universal mind in all people."[6] Aaron Copland said, "Inspiration may be a form of super-consciousness, or perhaps of subconsciousness — I wouldn't know. But I am sure that it is the antithesis of self-consciousness."[7]

The highest state a musician can be in is a *selfless state*. Just as a river bed receives the great waters, we receive inspiring ideas. For many, becoming such a channel is little more than a myth or wishful thinking. Artists often have trouble getting out of their own way, and they must therefore struggle. They are often swept away by a river of mental and emotional activity. They are drowning in feelings of inferiority, inadequacy, and anxiety – the battle is mistaken for a holy war and romanticized.

---

[6] The *Universal Mind Of Bill Evans: The Creative Process and Self Teaching*. Rhapsody Films Inc., 1991
[7] Copeland, Aaron. *Music and Imagination*. Cambridge: Harvard University Press, 1952.

But the struggle is simply with their ego. What should be an ecstatic act becomes as much fun as paying the monthly bills!

When I ask people which musician first attracted them to music, they often mention one who transcended these limitations. In the hands of such people, music has the potential of changing lives. Even when novices go to their concerts, they feel something opening inside. People can achieve this state in any kind of work, but they usually do not, because they don't regard their work as creative or "holy." After attending a concert containing this special feeling, they may be motivated to wait fifteen extra minutes before turning on the television upon arriving home. If the music had that effect, it was indeed important!

One of the attractions of art is the possibility it affords of opening the heart, of being exposed to a level of inspiration not usually experienced. It excites and delights. People all over the world have sought this experience in many ways. Some seek it by sailing or climbing mountains, and others by shooting heroin or eating sugar.

If you look at videos of artists such as Vladimir Horowitz, Miles Davis, Count Basie, Itzhak Perlman and others, you will see how they play from this space. After considering the material in this book, you'll view what they are doing in a new light. When Miles Davis approached the microphone, he focused himself into that space before playing the first note. There would frequently be long silences between his phrases. In that time, you could see and feel him re-centering himself. That is very rare in jazz musicians today. That practice has the paradoxical effect of heightening people's awareness and increasing the intensity of the moment. Miles Davis had the audience transfixed *before he played the first note!* Likewise, when Vladimir Horowitz played, you could see absolute stillness and concentration as he "watches his hands" play the piece.

To achieve that level of focus, there is no room for a cluttered mind; no room for doubt or worry. You never sense these masters thinking, "Gee, I sure hope I sound good for the folks out there!"

You know it when you see it. You know it when you hear it. The room electrifies quickly.

Miles was one of the best modern-day examples of the full power of the "master space." When he played, you didn't compare him to other trumpet players. You didn't even think of Miles as just a trumpet player. You speak of Miles when you're talking about spirits, about mystical experiences. When you speak of trumpet players, Dizzy Gillespie, Freddie Hubbard, Kenny Dorham, Fats Navarro and Wynton Marsalis come to mind. But when Miles played, you didn't think about what instrument he played so much as his aura, the sound of his band. Your eyes would follow him as he walked around the stage. He may not have played trumpet as well as those other people, but when he played his first note, we were in rapt attention. Others could play a thousand notes and not get our attention that way.

Keith Jarrett says,"Whatever clothes Miles wore, it was always Miles in those clothes. Whatever noise was around him, Miles still played from that need, his sound coming from that silence, the vast liquid, edgeless silence that existed before the first musician played the first note. We need this silence, because *that's* where the music is."[8]

False Idols

Jazz, as well as other types of music, has always been about the search for inspiration and the inner connection. This connection has been the treasure coveted or extolled by poets and artists throughout human history. In the nineteen twenties and thirties, many jazz musicians sought it with alcohol. In the forties, it was heroin, the new buzz. And what is the attraction of heroin? You *can't think,* you can only do. You can't play too much, you can only play what *wants to come out.* You accept everything that comes out without worry or pain. So, in their own way, those players were also searching for the "space." Even the great Charlie Parker felt this need. There are stories of him

[8]Jarrett, Keith. New York Times Article

arriving to a gig without his drug, not playing well, leaving the gig, copping some heroin, coming back and playing great.

This is not a recommendation to start shooting heroin; but it illustrates that the inner search in some form has always been prevalent in the artist. The first time Charlie Parker did heroin must have been exquisite! But the one great sin of all drugs is ... *the feeling doesn't last!* You always have to do more, getting less and less out of it. As you increase the dosage of whatever you're addicted to, be it violence or chocolate cheesecake – the result is always sad or even tragic. Early in his life, John Coltrane found heroin. A bit later, he used LSD. The psychedelic drugs of the sixties and seventies gave the user a different kind of experience. You got the buzz, but a window would also open that allowed you to go beyond physical reality and explore other realms of consciousness (similar to the "buzz" illustrated on those cereal commercials). In this state, the musician could see and hear on other levels. With heightened senses, it was possible to milk the ecstasy of each note. But after the effects of the drug wore off, the window always closed, making the natural state feel dry and intolerable. Eventually, for John Coltrane, the search led to no drugs. Toward the end of his life, his path had evolved into meditation, diet and spirituality. He ran the gamut, but was always searching for the same state. Finally he found what he was looking for within himself. The folly of human history is the search for this state in things outside us. This explains all wars, all quests for money, power, sex and other sensory experiences. The ultimate security one seeks can only be found within.

I play music from this space. The longer I play, the deeper into the 'space' I go and the quieter my mind becomes. Other issues seem less important. I focus deeper and deeper in the moment. Inspiration and ideas start to flow through me. The execution of the music becomes automatic. I find myself resting more and more as the music progresses. When it reaches the point of happening by itself, I am able to play all night. In fact, I have trouble stopping! I find that I love playing more now than when I was a kid, and the music coming out is more than I could have hoped for!

Don't waste your time moralizing about drugs and sex. It's not about being locked out of the Kingdom of Heaven. I believe that whatever force is the guiding principle of our existence, He/She wants us to feel *that good* all the time. That power has provided a nectar within our very own Selves. I capitalize "Self" because I was taught to capitalize the name of God. That's where I have come to believe He/She lives, in that inner space inside me. If we would just stand still and quiet ourselves long enough to sense that power, we would come to know an ecstasy that lasts. We must decide that it's more important to surrender to the space and to love what it gives than to play well. Once that decision is made, music will open herself to us and reveal all her secrets. We will experience waves of joy. Then we will become beacons that can light the way for others, and our mission will truly become important.

Practice

Perhaps music feels great as long as you're about fifteen feet away from the instrument, but as you move closer, a different energy takes over and your connection dwindles. It's like a horror movie where, from a distance, your bride looks beautiful, but as you get closer, the dress becomes tattered, her face shrivels up, her hair becomes dried and gray, the flowers wilt and all the petals fall off her bouquet; and by the time you reach her, she has turned into a hideous skeleton!

How can we retain the bliss of freedom as we approach our instrument? *We must let go of all desires and focus on love.* To have the nectar flow through us, we must honor our inner being, and practice receiving what is being given. We must practice and strengthen this connection daily. We may even have to go outside of music to do it. This is really important, because playing, being so addictive, pulls us easily from the true goal and draws us back into more mundane realms.

But when you have made the inner connection, playing becomes more like taking dictation from within. Work with the thought, *I am a master, I am great.* Then just put your hands on the instrument, trust them, and eventually it will be so.

"Do not fear mistakes. There are none."

— Miles Davis

Chapter 11
"There Are No Wrong Notes"

As you improvise from an expanded consciousness, you discover that, in fact, *there are no wrong notes!* Appropriateness and correctness are products of the mind. Trying to live within those imaginary guidelines inhibits the flow. I have illustrated this in clinics very clearly by playing *All The Things You Are* in two keys simultaneously. I'll play the chords in "Ab" and the lines in "A." Playing in those two keys should create many wrong notes. It should sound tremendously dissonant, but everyone is amazed to hear how fresh and stimulating it sounds! There is a secret here: if dissonant notes are played and the player embraces them as consonant, *the listener will also hear them as consonant!* Conversely, even the simplest harmony will sound strange to a listener if the player hasn't understood that harmony. If you listen to the wrong notes, meditate and embrace them with your heart, affirming their beauty, they will become sonic rubies, sparkling with tone. You can resolve so-called dissonant intervals the same way.

When a madman comes along to whom violence is consonant, his attitude may convince people that violence is beautiful. Followers go temporarily insane in his presence, falling prey to his complete self-acceptance! Later on, they might wonder how they could have fallen under that spell. Charles Manson had that mad man's conviction. His relationship to violence was like Monk's relationship to dissonance. Manson had such a love for violence that the people under his influence accepted his insanity. The same thing was certainly true of Hitler. People were so "inspired" by his message that they followed his lead. It's the inspiration itself we crave. When a person acts with complete confidence, even for insane purposes, it fills a void in us. Charismatic individuals make their followers do insane things by the force of their personalities. It proves the point that the force of a person's will, of his self-acceptance, can be so strong that he can change the view of the masses.

Musicians of every era, coming from that intuitive place, would use notes that the society of the time thought were insane. "One renowned pianist remembered the relief he felt during a performance when he missed the specific keys he intended to hit and Charlie Parker exclaimed, 'I hear you,' having interpreted the erroneous pitches within the pieces' framework as an 'interesting chord voicing.'[1] In the movie *Robin Hood*, Maid Marian says to Robin Hood, "You speak treason, my lord!" Robin Hood arrogantly replies, "Fluently!"

The visionary is often regarded as a heretic and the devil's tool. Through the force of his will and his sincere need of more intensity in the music, the musical visionary has convinced us time and time again that these dissonances were the new *right notes.* The heresy of the 14th century became the conventional wisdom of the 15th century. So the question is: if the notes sounded wrong and unusable in the 14th century, how did they become *desirable* in the 15th century? The answer is that they were never wrong! We just heard them that way. Hence, the truth: *there are no wrong notes.* There is a Zen saying: "Truth starts as heresy, grows into fashion, and decays into superstition."

Unrestrained by your prejudgments, your taste for consonance and dissonance shifts back and forth like the desire for hot and cold. What feels better after playing in the snow all day than a warm fire and some hot chocolate? But after sweating awhile and removing more and more clothes, doesn't going out into the cold air sound appealing? In the same way you would fluctuate between consonance and dissonance. After a period of playing "inside" the changes or chords of a tune, my ears delight

---

[1]Berliner Paul F. "Thinking in Jazz: Composing in the Moment." *Jazz Educators Journal*, May 1994. (p. 33).

in the sound of playing "outside" the changes. But as soon as I feel the responsibility to "play out," that becomes dull and boring, and I find playing the simplest, sweetest melody absolutely delicious. I never call myself modern or traditional, in or out, new or used, because I prefer not to be hemmed in by rigid definitions.

The Monk Principle

Thelonious Monk was a perfect example of a creator with a strong inner connection. His writing and playing were an extension of his personality, and he invented musical jokes that no one had ever thought of before. His compositions are obviously great, but think about his piano playing for a moment. He had a herky-jerky style, playing odd rhythms with a strange feel. His voicings weren't nearly as pretty as those of Bill Evans, nor could he create an easy groove like Red Garland or Wynton Kelly. For God's sake, Art Tatum was still alive! If it was just about piano playing, why would you listen to anyone other than Art Tatum? It was said of Monk that he could make a concert grand sound like an out-of-tune upright. There were certainly better pianists around in his day. So why was Thelonious Monk so revered? The answer is that he had the *depth of sound, the arrogance to play what he wanted to play.* He was uninhibited by mind and fortified by spirit. Behind every note was the belief that "this is the truth." He didn't believe in wrong notes. He believed that they were right notes because *he played them.*

Do you believe that every note you play is right, or are you always looking for the right notes? The world is made up of two kinds of people: the ones who play the right stuff, and the ones who are *looking* for the right stuff to play! Miles Davis was always making the next right note out of the last wrong note. Monk had so much conviction in what he played (perhaps enjoying the moral indignation of the establishment), that while he was playing, we couldn't conceive of anything else. He had the same effect on his audience as the madmen described earlier. The authenticity of Monk came from the permission he gave himself to be a genius, to take scraps of junk that most of us wouldn't know what to do with and to proclaim, "This is beautiful."And yet today, when one plays a Monk tune, one instinctively tries to play like Monk. There are many young pianists who can play piano more efficiently than Monk did, but when playing a Monk tune, they try to *devolve* their playing to sound like Monk. That's how powerful his statement was: they can't hear anything else!

However, you can't get power from being Monk; it comes from being yourself. That's the only way a person can summon that kind of strength. You can never get it by recreating. You have to *create. For music to be real, it has to come from a deeper place than the "little mind" and we can hear the difference!*

Mind — Behave!

As you play, there must be no intellectual interference. Intellect is good for picking out an instrument, teaching or getting to the gig on time. It's good for academia, it's good for practicing scales, reading books and studying. But it is not good for creating. Intellect has to surrender to instinct when it's time to play.

I have often looked around me on stage and viewed with amusement how others were caught up in a drama of their own making. It was a very transcendent feeling.

Most of us think that the license to create is for others, *not for us*. But inspired people show us by example what is possible for everyone.

William Blake said, "Jesus was all virtue, and acted from impulse not from rules."[2] That description sounds a lot like Monk and Miles! Imagine the rarefied air Louis Armstrong must have breathed when he and his contemporaries were developing, without precedent, what would become jazz. It's as though there is a cosmic bank somewhere in the universe where the great ones have their accounts. The currency is unlimited creativity and ideas. The rest of us are always trying to borrow from their

---

[2] William Blake, *The Marriage of Heaven and Hell*. London, 1793.

accounts. I don't wish to borrow – *I want to open my own account!* I don't want to play the way Monk played, *I want to feel the way Monk felt* when he played. I like to feel that no one has ever played this instrument before me; that it's like a blank stone for God to emblazon his commandments on. And there can be new testaments every day!

"That's The Most Beautiful Sound I've Ever Heard"

Some brain-washing is necessary here — not in the sense of mind-control, but in the sense that "My brain is really filthy, it needs a good washing!" When I drop my hands on the piano, no matter what comes out, I say, *"That is the most beautiful sound I've ever heard."* Try it on your own instrument. Play a note, and before you have time to evaluate it, proclaim, *"That is the most beautiful sound I've ever heard."* Will you be oppressed by the judgments of good and bad, or will you delight in *"That is the most beautiful sound I've ever heard?"* Which is true? *Neither,* in the objective sense. Sound is neither good or bad, beautiful or ugly. We superimpose those values onto it. Or both statements are true, depending on what you believe. Which belief shall you embrace? It should be the *one that best serves your creativity! You will find yourself far more free and powerful if you assume that all notes you play are the most beautiful sounds you've ever heard!*

This attitude might make you a bit crazy, but it instills a brilliance that makes your music shine. You will joyously receive ideas without narrowing the channel from which music may pour through you.

Wanting to play well and wanting to make an "inner connection" are often contradictory goals. Sometimes it is absolutely necessary to allow yourself to play what your intellect calls "bad music" so that the inner connection can be established.

Saying, *"There are no wrong notes"* or *"Every note I play is the most beautiful sound I've ever heard"* may sound bit like New Age philosophy, but Miles Davis had another way of putting it:

"This is the baddest ____ you ever heard, and if you don't think so, I'm going to kick your __!" That was his way of saying, "*Every note I play is the most beautiful sound I've ever heard.*"

Beboppers also tended to be less than philosophical about it, and the issue would often be resolved with fists or even knives and guns! But even though they were not always the nicest people, the essence of their strength contained this same principle. They had full confidence in what they were about to play. This allowed them to form a link to a deeper part of themselves and directly tap the inner waves of inspiration. It must also be said that a person may have great mastery in their music and even possess impressive spiritual power and *not be a nice person!*

The point is: you too can have permission to believe in yourself – but that permission has to come from you. No one will give it to you until they see that you already have it. Let us meditate on this.

Chapter 12

Meditation #1

(Please listen to Meditation #1 on CD)

I am great. I am a master.

$\mathcal{P}$ut your feet squarely on the floor ... Take a nice deep breath ... Take a good one. Don't cheat yourself. Give yourself a beautiful deep breath. Take another deep breath, and breathe it out slowly. As we go through our lives, day by day, the most essential thing is breath, yet we tend to take small ones (a clue that something's wrong). Right now, on this beautiful day in your life, breathe in deeply ... Breathe in your own self ... Breathe in your own greatness. This very day, commit yourself to reclaiming the greatness inside you. Breathe in and connect with the seat of your power and magnificence.

Take another deep breath and really enjoy it, as if I had said, "Have another piece of pie." Imagine I baked a big delicious pie. The piece I gave you really wasn't big enough, and you just have to have some more. Right now, treat the air like that. Treat your next breath as if it were a craving. Begin to relax.

Start to feel your body relaxing. Feel relaxation from the top of your head on down ... If any clothing you're wearing is uncomfortably tight, loosen it a bit. Loosen your belt if necessary. Take off your shoes if they bother you in any way. Make yourself as comfortable as possible. Let this moment be a holiday from perpetual discomfort.

Take another deep breath, and exhale slowly ... and another deep breath ... and exhale slowly. Now relax your head and your face ... let your cheeks relax, and your jaw ... and let your eyes relax, and your mouth ... tongue ... throat ... and ears ... let them relax and imagine the canals are getting wider and wider, until your whole head ... disappears.

Relax your neck ... and your shoulders. Many of you feel a lot of tension in your neck and shoulders because the enemy, fear, keeps them tense. Fear of people ... fear of playing ... fear of sounding bad ... fear of not surviving ... fear of not being well thought of ... fear of not being a successful musician ... all this registers itself in the neck and shoulders. Even though you may not be able to rid yourself of this tension, just notice it and be willing to let it go.

As you breathe, notice any pain you feel and just let it go. If it persists, then just observe it. Step back and observe it as if it were someone else's body. Do that with each part of your body as it is mentioned.

Now relax your shoulder blades ... your chest ... your upper back .... breathe deeply as you focus on the muscles and the bones and the rib cage, and just let them go ... let them drop. Imagine you were gripping these muscles tightly in your hand ... and then imagine relaxing your grip, opening your hand, and releasing them as you would release a bird into flight.

Relax your stomach ... lower back ... and your spine. Now try to sense your inner organs. Relax your liver ... your kidneys ... your lungs. See if you can sense your heart muscle. Sense where it is in your chest. Right now, relax that muscle. Keep breathing deeply and relax even more.

Feel your hips relax ... let them hang loose ... and your buttocks ... thighs ... knees ... your calves ... your ankles ... and your feet. Your feet are usually abused by tight shoes, walking, curling your toes while playing, as well as fear. Fear lodges itself in the feet. Stretch your toes out and then let them just relax.

Take another deep breath and send that breath through your whole body. Hear that breath going in and coming out. Let yourself descend into the deepest, most relaxed place inside your body ...

We are establishing a connection from your innermost self to your instrument. From this day forward, we will practice that direct linkage. Begin to focus on your mind ...

Naturally, there are a lot of questions that arise. How could I function from this meditative space? How can I play in time without getting lost? How can I possibly practice at all? The answers to these questions will come, but for now, let us let go of all questions. Relax the mind and observe the thoughts that might be going through it. If there are no thoughts, then are you truly blessed! That is heaven on earth. But if you are having thoughts, don't try to stop them, just observe ... as you observe your thoughts, you might find that your mind is quieting down. Take a breath and let go of the *need to play well* ... take another breath, and release all pressures to play music ... release *the need to play music* ... just for a moment ... it won't hurt you ... *you can have all your obsessions back right after this exercise!* ... but for right now ... just let it all go ...

Now take another very deep breath and blow out any more thoughts of limitation or negativity. Imagine an incredibly bright light shooting into the top of your head, filling every cell of your head with warmth. This healing light is filling your head, just as a fish bowl is filled with water or a balloon is filled with air. Feel this very bright light entering your neck and shoulders. Imagine it warming every cell in each part of the body of which I speak. The light is now filling your chest and back. Feel the light running down your spine like a bolt of lightning, shooting all the way down to the base of your spine and exploding out through your back and vertebrae. Imagine the light filling your stomach, buttocks and hips, and shooting down your legs. Feel it shooting out of every toe like lasers. Now imagine light pouring down your neck and shoulders, pouring like molten lava into your arms and forearms and wrists and hands. That light is now shooting out of every finger like lasers ... shooting out of your eyes, ears, mouth, nostrils, fingertips, toes and every pore of your body. Light is pouring through your body, and you are an *empty vehicle* for this light.

Let yourself imagine it all. Don't worry if it's true, or if it's working; just *make believe*. Imagine the light is getting brighter and brighter ... hotter and hotter ... and ... now ... you ... disappear! All that is left is light!

Take another deep breath and take in the light as a fish takes in water through its gills. Let yourself become very comfortable in this space. Imagine that it is not some special place you can only go to in meditation, but this is who you really are. Imagine that this is your *real self*.

Inhale this thought: *"I am perfect, I am a master."* And as you exhale, release any thought of unworthiness ... Again, inhale the thought, *"I am a master ."* Exhale any feeling of negativity or low value. Imagine you are blowing out any darkness left inside. And with every inhalation comes the thought, *"I am great, I am a master."*

This new image of yourself may be uncomfortable. We're quite comfortable with our limitations. But right now, put the message in every cell of your body and mind: *"I am great, I am a master."* Scan your body and mind for any remaining negativity, and release it with an exhalation, saying, *"I am great, I am a master."*

Go to the very center of your being ... and breathe in the idea, *"I am a master, I am great."* Repeat it several times softly to yourself. *"I am a master, I am very great."* Let this thought become more and more comfortable. Let it seem more normal every second, not special, not unusual. *I am a master. I am very great. Everything I do is great. Every note I play has greatness.* Let this feeling take over your whole being.

Surrender ... give up your imperfections now. Don't wait until Monday. Don't wait until 2:00 on Saturday. Do it now. Become the master you already are ... now. It is the truth that you are already perfect. Surrender to this truth. You are what you think. Fill your head with this fragrance, *I am very great.*

When you do things with limited beliefs, they manifest limited results. So right now, start a practice and maintain it every day for the rest of your life. For just a few moments a day, you will remind yourself, *I am great. I am a master. I don't need my actions to prove this to me, I start my day with this belief.* Take another deep inhalation ...

Rest in the knowledge of your greatness. Breathe ... deeply ... and exhale ... slowly ... releasing all thoughts ... and loving yourself ... acknowledging the master inside you ... Do not think of it as outside yourself, but as a reality you've never perceived. You don't have to do anything to be great. It is a fact. You were born great, and you've never lost your greatness for a single second. Let this new thought be a place of rest. Imagine that we've just made a lovely bed for you. A warm, soft bed with big fluffy pillows, and as you sink down into it, you sink into your own greatness.

Finally, let's practice, one more time, without any doubts, without embracing any rational arguments to the contrary; pretend fully with all your imagination, like a child might: *"I am perfect. I am great. I am a master."*

Chapter 13
Effortless Mastery

The term "effortless mastery" is actually redundant because mastery *is* the effortless execution of music. It does not refer to how many things one can do, but rather the quality with which one does anything. If something can be done perfectly, every time, without thought, it is said to be mastered.

The jazz master unconsciously calls upon a wealth of information from which he improvises his solos. The classical master performs all aspects of the piece – fingering, dynamics, and all the correct notes – without thought. At performance time, the music *plays itself* while the musician *observes*.

Being a master of improvised music does not mean that one is able to play every style or every kind of tune. It doesn't mean being a good Latin player and fusion player, as well as playing great bebop, although such a person may be called a master of styles. The term mastery doesn't refer to playing complex chord changes such as John Coltrane's *Giant Steps*, or being able to play *Flight of the Bumble Bee.*

Mastery is playing whatever you're capable of playing ... every time ... WITHOUT THINKING ...

That is why the great ones can do what they do every night without faltering. *It is that easy.* Why do certain jazz artists "burn" every night on every solo? Because burning comes easily to them. They may drool when they speak, have trouble writing their names or tying their shoelaces, but at the instrument, *they burn!*

There are masters of different aspects of music. For example, Wynton Kelly was a master of the groove. He didn't have the chordal development that Bill Evans had, but the way he danced on the groove was transcendent mastery. Miles Davis couldn't play all the notes that Dizzy Gillespie could, but he was a master of deep space, phrasing, and expression. To be perceived as a master, one must stay within the boundaries of what comes naturally and easily. After we hear a great musician, we might be tempted to reach for things that we do not yet understand and play over our heads. It is at that precise moment that we lose our way or lose the inner connection. Tension and pressure have replaced the flow. Ironically, it is when we are trying to sound brilliant that we stumble, whereas when we stay within ourselves, we sound better. There is always a schism between what the ego wants to play and what wants to come out. Although the master player may have great technical ability, you will not sense his attempt to show it; the technique manifests unconsciously. Many of our favorite artists are not overwhelming technicians, but make deep statements. Others may be technical marvels, but we criticize their lack of expression. In Jazz, we have examples of musicians who may not be on the cutting edge technically, but who are undoubtedly masters of *pure music*. While listening to them, you can't conceive of any other way to play.

In sports, it often happens that the team with less "stars" wins it all. The players or coach will always talk about "staying within themselves," or "just doing what they can do." In improvised music, the one who stays within himself may be perceived as a master.

The apex of impressive artistry is the ability to perform technically advanced music with the same ease and inspiration as a simple folk song. If one combines masterful technique with the "channeling" of inspiration directly from within, the result can be awesome (I regard the execution of scales, chords, dynamics and expression as being "technical"). After all is mastered, the inner being may manifest, unimpeded by the vehicle's (i.e., the performer's) lack of knowledge. In this light, training oneself to the highest possible level may be regarded as an act of worship to that inner being.

Effortless Execution

For something to be mastered on your instrument, it must feel as simple as *playing one note*. Whether or not you're a pianist, go to the piano and just drop your finger on one note. Notice how easy and thoughtless that is. Even the most difficult passages in classical music should feel this sure-handed. Actually, we have many examples of effortless mastery in our lives – we just don't consider them very astounding. For example, we are all masters of using a fork. You could be talking, making love and doing your taxes and you'd never misuse a fork. In all the hundreds of thousands of times you have used a fork, did you ever miss your mouth? Did you ever poke yourself in the eye or stick it in your ear? Nope, bullseye every time! That's the way it feels to have mastered musical material. Professional improvisers, whether Indian tabla players or be-bop saxophonists, can always access their language in this way.

Practice To Perfection

How well should the material be learned? I compare this to a tightrope walker in the circus. He has to learn to walk the rope so well that he could never make a mistake. It has to be easy for him to do it, no matter how hard it looks to the audience. If it is easy, he will perform perfectly every time without much effort. On the other hand, if he learned to walk the tight rope the way some of us have learned to play, he'd be dead by now!

Every instrumentalist makes a case for why his particular instrument requires effort. Again I am reminded of the circus. I once saw the Cirque du Sol, a wonderful circus that also features music and choreography. Their acts are very exciting and unusual. While the performers were engaged in amazing feats, I watched their faces and noticed that through it all, they were so calm, either smiling at the audience or at each other while their bodies were in such incredible motion that they created optical illusions! I can guarantee that what I saw was at least as hard as playing the trumpet, yet they performed flawlessly for nine or ten shows a week and made it look easy.

If one's life depends on doing something right, as in the case of the tightrope walker, one will practice on a much deeper level. But in fact, many students and professionals are not properly rehearsed in the basics, and so for them music seems much more difficult to play. There are many reasons for this improper preparation. The educational system is partially responsible. As I stated before, we are rushed along through one concept after another (not to mention all the unrelated things we have to study that take time and focus away from mastering music). Only a relatively small percentage of students make it through those hurdles. Many fall by the wayside who might otherwise succeed. But the main culprit is the dysfunctional, fear-based practicing I referred to earlier. That "little voice in your head" won't let you stay with a subject long enough to master it.

Unfamiliar, Not Difficult

It is good to view things as familiar or unfamiliar, rather than as difficult or easy. If you give yourself the message, "This is difficult," the piece may discourage you, and it will still be difficult to play even after you've learned it. However, if you believe that *all music is easy,* then you'll assume that you are unfamiliar with the piece because *"it hasn't become easy yet."*

Sometimes you hear yourself botching things up that you've practiced, and you don't even question it. That's because the mistakes actually agree with your belief that *"I am not a master,"* or *music is hard."* In fact, the material has not been practiced to the proper level of ease. **Music has to become easy. That's the secret!**

A perfect example can be found in the jazz standard, *All The Things You Are.* What is the most difficult part of that tune? Many musicians would answer that it's the second half of the bridge (the middle part of the tune). Why should that be? It is just II-V-I (a basic chord progression), but it's in the key of E major. So what's the problem? Is one less talented in E major? Less creative? Is E major a harder key? Or is it just *less familiar?* That's the answer. Jazz players don't play in that key very often (unless they play guitar). A lack of familiarity makes it seem more difficult because we simply haven't practiced that key. Therefore, we fumble looking for the right notes, lose the groove, and our freedom is shattered. For non-musicians who are *unfamiliar* with what I'm talking about, the main point is that things that have not been mastered seem more difficult than they are. Maybe you delayed buying a computer for many years because of how difficult it seemed to be to use. That's the same idea.

Master One Thing First

You should stay with one exercise until mastery has been achieved. For example, when you practice one line over chords in a difficult key, there are many lessons to be absorbed: the difficult key, the chords, a line that makes more sense than the lines you can play in time, the required rhythmic intensity, the technique and fingering needed to play the line very fast, and the exposure of little glitches that inhibit your playing in general.

It is possible to focus on the "space" while practicing a line and wait for "it" to execute itself perfectly (I will discuss how to do this in the later chapters).

If you did this, many things would improve during the patient practice of this one line. Upon reaching your goal, you would hear yourself playing this one phrase on the level of great players. This would inspire you and give you the confidence that *you might become one of them some day*. You would start expecting that level in other exercises, and notice how improved your playing was in general. Achieving such mastery is like climbing a mountaintop and beholding a new vista. Now you know it's there and that you are capable of reaching it. You achieve an ease of playing that reinforces the message, *"I am a master. Music is easy!"*

Mastering The Ego

We must illuminate the ego's ruses and see how it sabotages our progress. I think that everyone would agree with this concept of practicing and playing, so why won't we do it? As I said before, it is because we are in a hurry – we need to sound good today, in our quest for a good self-image. We aren't in touch with our own inner beauty and so we seek it in our level of play. Self-centeredness, which some musicians suffer from in the extreme, is the wall between us and mastery.

This is why the initial practice in this book does not involve music as much as it does centering oneself on the more vast inner space, building an inner structure that will support, not derail, the concentration required to reach the goal. This mode of practicing allows the player to reach heights that his ego could only fantasize about.

Technical Mastery Creates Freedom

As previously discussed, there may be emotional and spiritual barriers to effortless playing. But a lack of technical mastery in the various elements of music may be another reason why we can't let go. You may be flying through an inspired solo when suddenly a gap in your training sends you crashing back to earth! Stream of consciousness is stopped in its tracks because you have to ask, "Where is the next note?" Nothing puts a crimp in spontaneity more than a momentary lapse in knowledge. Most of us never get past the stage of struggling with technique. But we can never experience our deeper feelings in music if we still have to think about rhythm, phrasing, form or the chord changes. The struggle is often attributed to a lack of talent, but it is usually due to a gap — something not learned properly. Seeking new levels of technical mastery should be a life long pursuit – not because you want to impress, but to facilitate any direction the great spirit inside you wants to go.

A teacher once told her student to master technique so that he could "soar with the divinity of music." Isn't that beautiful? Once after I played a concert, an interviewer asked me, "If you could add anything to your playing, what would it be?" Without hesitation, I answered, "More technique." He looked at me strangely, because I had shown a lot of different skills in this performance and that didn't seem to be my most pressing need. Also, it was not the most politically-correct answer. He asked why, and I replied, "Because I love to let the great spirit manifest through me. She only gets stuck when I go for something that's not there technically. That distracts me from the bliss I am receiving."

Rhythm

In America and parts of Europe, the most common gap is a lack of rhythm. We live in a culture that externalizes rhythm by teaching it too late in life. Children growing up in households that play rhythmic music tend to grow up more rhythmic, of course. Effortless mastery of rhythm occurs in certain cultures where it is an integral part of life. In Brazil, the children's first musical experiences are rhythmic. In America, they tend to be more melodic. Is it an accident that the Brazilian people are more naturally rhythmic than we are? I lived with a Brazilian family for a while and at the dinner table, family members would pick up knives and forks and play samba rhythms on the glasses and plates. They always sounded good. I don't think I met anyone in Brazil who was intimidated by rhythm. They knew their various rhythms the way we know our nursery rhymes.

Rhythmic mastery might be more important than harmonic mastery because in jazz, weak melodies and harmonies will sound strong when played with strong rhythm, but even good melodies and harmonies will sound anemic with weak rhythm. For example, some Latin and Afro-Cuban music features the simplest harmony; however, this harmony serves as a vehicle for rhythmic development that is thrilling to hear and see! The music we grow up with will be the most familiar, and therefore the easiest to master. It is a shame that the music we absorb as children, particularly in white America, is so devoid of rhythm (e.g. Christmas carols). It must also be said that most classical players *lack a basic sense of rhythm.* They may have a method of negotiating the most complex rhythms of modern music, but I have been shocked many times at the average string player's inability to play an eighth-note anticipation (a rhythm that anticipates the next bar by one eighth-note). There would be incredible benefits for classical musicians if rhythm classes of all kinds were mandatory in their conservatories. If they had an inner pulse while playing Bartok and Stravinsky, we would hear orchestras that really burn! For them, and for many of us, years of rhythmic indoctrination are in order.

Form

Mastery of form enables one to state form in an increasingly subtle manner. The more the form becomes second nature, the more it becomes a vehicle for free improvisation. That is what we call "stretching." But the desire to be "complex" often drives the musician to a forced attempt to stretch. The result is typically ungrooving, self-conscious music, if not losing one's place in the beat altogether! When I learn a new tune, especially if it has rough spots for me, I often play it for a long time before I learn another one. I stay with the tune and usually don't perform it with my trio until I have "transcended" its form and changes (unless it's a gig that I feel I can practice on). Only then do I take it out of the oven, so to speak. Although I can probably play it fine the first time, I want to reach the level of playing that I am accustomed to before moving on. Only then do I feel as though I'm saying something, using the form of the tune to express myself. Bill Evans described his tunes as vehicles; they are vehicles for self-expression, or expression of the "self."

You can learn more from penetrating the form of one tune than you can by merely "memorizing" many tunes. In the latter case, all you'll do is stumble through the changes, and the level of your playing will not rise. But through deep immersion in that one tune, you will *evolve to another level of playing!* You will then come to expect that level in other situations.

The Classical

In classical music, the notes are predetermined. How does this concept apply?

Just as the jazz instrumentalist falters improvising on chords in a strange key, so may the classical musician falter as an interpreter of passages that have not been adequately absorbed. *This happens to both types of musicians for the same reason: with overloaded minds, they rush through their material!*

The lapses in familiarity usually occur later in the piece, almost never in the first eight bars. This is because the player exhibits the most patience at the beginning of a piece. Typically, he starts from the beginning, so that part becomes most familiar. But as he advances, he loses patience, and a small voice in his head hurries him along with the thought that *there is so much else to practice!* He loses consciousness and overlooks the little glitches that are appearing like roaches in the kitchen. If he gets it right once or twice, he rationalizes that he knows it. It doesn't have the cozy feeling of the first eight bars, but he doesn't have time to notice that. When he performs the piece, he will always struggle at the same exact points, because he has only partially learned them. The goal of effortless mastery has not been realized. He never spends enough time slowly and comfortably moving his fingers through the passages. Soon he is hurrying through the passages again and again, giving his mind and body a message of anxiety and discomfort. The message of ease was never adequately sent.

Every time I practice written music, I move slowly enough to play it correctly, while almost in a state of meditation. In that way, I am teaching my fingers to perform by themselves while I soar! The classical player is often required to learn so much in such a short span of time that he practices as if to stave off disaster. Even if the player manages to negotiate troubled waters, he will play with a strain and effort that falls short of greatness.

That greatness, which he is programmed not to expect anyway, could be his if he would wait for effortlessness to arrive. He might not be ready for a recital very quickly, but his level of playing would improve with each piece he absorbed, in fact, *with every bar*. Like the improviser, he would find that one composition learned on the master level will have more meaning than an entire program learned the ordinary way.

Mastery of Sound

Another quality of mastery is the absolute wisdom with which the artist expresses his notes. They may be simple, but they resonate in a profound way. This depth of tone or phrase has to do with the artist's "inner mastery" of the sounds he's playing. It reflects the character of the player as an evolved being, and the depth with which he unites himself to his notes. He contemplates the different sounds, and forms personal relationships with intervals, chords, rhythms, and so on.

For example, one would think that if two people play the same piano, it should sound the same, because the piano's sound is made through the arbitrary device of a hammer hitting a string. Yet those same notes will have a very different sound from one player to another. I'll never forget attending Bill Evans' fiftieth birthday party. I won't mention any names, but there were more pianists in one room than I can ever remember seeing before. I felt like I was attending a dictator's convention! The pianist who threw the party owned a grand piano. (The piano will also remain nameless.) It was a decent piano, but it sounded bright and metallic, as that particular brand often can. Various young luminaries sat down to play for Bill during the party. They sounded great, and the piano sounded bright and metallic as expected. Then Bill sat down to play, and a miraculous change in the sound took place. Suddenly we were listening to a Steinway B recorded in 1958! The piano seemed to have that dark richness that had become increasingly rare in pianos and even more rare in the touch of young pianists. At one point, he played a duet with another pianist, and the two halves of the piano actually sounded different! If he played the upper register, the piano sounded dark and beautiful there, and bright and chunky on the bottom. When he played the bottom, there was an opposite effect. For me, this was dramatic example of the inner relationship to sound.

I believe there are basically two reasons for Bill's perfect sound under all circumstances. He had perfectly weighted arms with wrists like shock absorbers, so that he could always achieve force without banging; and because of the deep and thorough process by which he absorbed his material, *his hands always knew perfectly well where they were going.* With calm certainty, they would perform what they had been programmed to perform. In this way, his hands didn't need to *lunge* for the notes; they were always right there. His calm focus led him to play what he understood, rather than to reach for things outside his experience. For this reason, his playing always sounded perfect. His sound was the envy of classical and jazz pianists alike. We took it for granted that all the notes would be perfect.

At the party, one of the pianists asked him what he practiced, and he gave us a glimpse at his process. Like one of his musical phrases, his answer was very succinct. "I practice the minimum." He meant the *minimum amount of material, not time.* For me, this was a complete confirmation that focusing on a small amount of material, getting inside it, investigating all its variations, running it through different keys. In short, *mastering it* was what separated Bill Evans from so many others. It was his pathway to mastery.

Mastering the Body

Questions arise such as: "The act of playing instruments takes effort. How can one be effortless while doing it?," or "How does one play fast tempos from this relaxed space?"

The answer can be found by looking at martial arts. Those disciplines require great concentration rather than strength. To focus the body's energy into one act, there is no *extraneous* tension. That's the key. Most musicians play while holding tension in parts of their bodies that don't need to be tense. That tension is the result of their basic relationship to playing: a pattern of struggle. In karate, to break a board, you have to be very focused and very relaxed. Doesn't that seem like a contradiction? How can you be very relaxed and break a board? You have to be so focused that your movement happens by itself. There is great tension, but it is purposeful tension focused exactly where it is needed. You must have the faith that once you start moving, *it's going to happen.* If there is any doubt, the thing that will break will not be the board. If there is fear before the act, that cracking sound might be your bones. Focusing on that level is achieved by absolute relaxation. Herrigel describes this in *Zen In The Art Of Archery,* when he observes his master shoot an arrow. "At least in the case of the Master the loose [releasing of the arrow] looked so simple and undemanding that it might have been child's play."[1]

We're not talking about the kind of relaxation you experience slouched in a chair watching the football game. We're talking about *relaxed focus* — having the discipline to perform arduous tasks while remaining soft and supple on the inside, as muscles not needed for the task are at rest, and the mind is tranquil. This is the intent and spirit of yoga.

If you allow your body to learn without interference from your mind, it will learn what it needs to perform the task. The knowledge that the body has arises at just the right time spontaneously. It knows instinctively how to move. When practicing or playing is forced, you tend to use more muscles than are necessary. The muscles that are needed are also used inefficiently. For example, most saxophonists use much more effort than needed. They strain facial muscles that are not needed for the production of tone. Their facial contortions are often an attempt to *coerce* the music. All you need are the muscles of your embouchure, your lungs, hands and arms. Everything else could be completely at rest or in rapt attention. The back should

[1]Eugen Herrigel, *Zen In The Art Of Archery* p. 20.

be balanced to allow all the body parts to hang from it. If the strap is properly adjusted, the player barely has to hold the instrument. The saxophone can actually become "uncomfortably easy" to play if you're not used to such efficiency. One can do more with less effort. And how many pianists have their shoulders raised up to their ears even while playing a ballad? What purpose do the shoulders serve in that position, except as a depository for fear?

People ask if this means that they have to stay still when they play. Of course not. That would be yet another restriction. In performance, if you want to dance, dance. If you want to scream, scream – for *we never edit ourselves while playing!* There is a point, however, where moving becomes a crutch, and one cannot function properly without it. For example, some pianists have to sing their lines and tap their feet or they cannot play clear, clean lines. In this case, *the fingers lack the rhythm in themselves and need coercion from external sources.* Even if you love to move in concert, it would be good to practice this efficiency of movement and stillness of the body at home. Then, while performing in any manner, that body-knowledge will support whatever you want to do.

If you center yourself before approaching the instrument, your body will discover this efficiency instinctively. Once I was teaching a bass player who could not play without stomping his feet as well as leaning over to "dig in." Since he was getting the beat from stomping his feet, he slowed down as his foot got tired. As I said, it's okay to dance and move with joy, but it's not good to *have to stamp your foot to keep time.* I asked him to stand upright, plant his feet on the floor, and let his arms hang down and relax. Then, I put the bass in his hands. He instantly looked more in control. I asked him to play using just his hands, which were now supported by his arms, which were supported by his back. He immediately played better without slowing down, while using *one-third of the energy.* He was relaxed and alert, and could look around at the other musicians and get involved in the music. If being centered had been his priority all along, *he would have slipped into this position automatically!*

111

While working with another bass player during a lesson, I noticed that his playing felt labored and uninspired. I saw that he was standing on the balls of his feet and shifting from side to side. His eyes were closed, but to me this did not signify deep absorption in the music. It indicated tension and desire, and he seemed overwhelmed by the acoustic bass. I said to him, "You were an electric bass player first, weren't you?" This statement surprised him. It was true and I'm sure he wondered how I knew that. The answer was that the upright bass seemed massive in his hands, and he dealt with it that way. I got him to stand back on his heels in a yoga-like mountain pose and root himself into the floor. Then I told him to take his mind off his playing completely and stare at my eyes – an exercise I do with many students. This causes them to lose consciousness of themselves (the same effect can be achieved by staring into a mirror). I told him to absorb himself completely in my eyes, while his hands played the bass *by themselves*. He immediately had flashes of a new, improved and effortless groove. The difference was quite dramatic, and we both laughed!

In yoga, while surrendering to your inner self, or to God, consumed with devotion, knowledge of your body's natural position arises spontaneously. With few exceptions, great players assume the most beneficial posture for channeling music. Recently, a trumpet player who studied with me said that he had taken a real good lesson with a famous trumpet teacher. I asked him what he had learned. He said that the main point had to do with his posture: he extended his head forward when he played. The teacher told him to keep his head back, which felt much easier. I reminded him that when he went into "the space," relieving his body of all tension and letting go of his mind, his head naturally did that. So you see, you can rehearse choreography of isolated body parts and not quite know why you're doing it, or you can journey to the source of all movement: spontaneous yoga or spontaneous balance — the place that puts your body into alignment so as to serve the goal of mastery. Simply go into the space, and add the horn to it. You get much more from dealing with the cause than the effect; and, because of all else that you receive from this center, **your very soul may reveal itself through the music.**

Mastery is Available to Everyone

This should be good news for many of you, because you may have thought that only people like Miles Davis and Thelonious Monk are allowed to be masters. When you speak, you improvise all the time, spouting your ideas freely in perfect sentences. *The same freedom is available with the language of music.* It's true that it comes to some people more easily, but mastery comes to all who wait for it. The ego may taunt you with thoughts like, *"You should have learned that by now,"* or *"You should be playing better by now,"* but focused work habits, determination, and a positive outlook will compensate for talent to a surprising degree. The specially talented are blessed (or cursed?) by the ease with which they can imbibe music, but greatness is not their exclusive property. In fact, many people with extraordinary talent have failed to achieve greatness precisely because they could never focus and lacked discipline. I'm reminded of Donald Erb's comment to me that "the bars are full of incredibly talented people."

Pete Rose, the baseball player, is an example of how hard work and attitude can overcome average talent. He will be the first to say that he was not especially gifted; but he made up for it with a ferocious desire to win and very thorough work habits. As a result, he accumulated more hits than anyone else who ever played the game.

The Result: Connection to All Wisdom

People are always asking me if I studied yoga, Zen, or tai chi, which for years, I did not, although in recent years (from the time of this writing) I have become a student of Siddha Yoga meditation. I've simply decided that effortlessness would be my prime consideration, that anything not played from an effortless place *is not worth playing.* I don't get my technique from studying technique. I get it from *letting my hands and arms find their way without my interference.* In doing so, I have unwittingly connected with the wisdom of the ancients. As I now read the writings of the great sages, I realize that I am on the same path, having the experiences they describe. Effortlessness allows us to become our own teachers, paving the way to mastery. If you get nothing else from this book, hopefully you'll at least walk away with the realization that effort gets in the way of great playing. *Effort and / or lack of preparation blocks true mastery.*

There was a great example of perfect, effortless motion on (of all places) television. One morning there was a live broadcast of Vladimir Horowitz performing in Moscow. Preceding the actual performance was a documentary of his historic return to his homeland. He had not been there in sixty years! Needless to say, there had been many sweeping changes in the Soviet Union during that time. His return was not popular with the Communist regime of Leonid Brezhnev.

As Horowitz arrived at the airport, there were members of his extended family waiting whom he had never met. A cousin who had been four years old when he had left the Soviet Union was now sixty-four! This was, to say the least, an emotional return. The government was not eager to highlight a performance by a "capitalist traitor," and did no promotion for his concert. There was only a simple poster on the wall of the Moscow Conservatory of Music on the day of the performance which read, "Vladimir Horowitz (USA)." Only one poster! 400 seats were available to the general public which were quickly swept up. The other 1800 seats were reserved for government officials and diplomats. There were hundreds more people waiting outside in the rain with their umbrellas. They remained there during the performance just to be near his energy. The concert itself was being broadcast live throughout the world. I think it was fair to say that, given all these factors, there was pressure!

Horowitz came out on stage to a standing ovation. Then he just sat there for a while and gazed into the audience. As everyone settled down, you could tell that he was also settling down: letting

114

all the emotions, all the nerves, all the political implications subside in his mind so that mastery could emerge, and his hands would perform what they had been trained to do so well. Watching him unburden himself in this way was electrifying for me, because I understood what he was doing.

Then, with no warning, his hands began playing the Scarlatti Sonata in E Major. The camera work was wonderful. First, it showed a long shot of him, then zoomed in on his face. He was the picture of concentration. Without seeing his hands, you could hear the music, but you wouldn't have thought he was playing. He looked like a kindly old man waiting for a bus. Then they showed his hands, and that was the strangest thing. No matter how difficult the music was, no matter how fast or slow, no matter what the challenge, the hands looked as though they were hardly moving! They looked like little animals peacefully grazing along the keys. The picture was disorienting because there was absolutely no effort. He was just observing his hands playing the music. What sublime sound they produced, so many colors! He had absorbed the written music to the point of mindlessness, with enough expression to intoxicate the gods! I use a video of this concert frequently in my clinics so that everyone can see and hear a clear manifestation of mastery.

Many of the same traits are evident in a video titled *Bill Evans on the Creative Process*. It was hosted by Bill's brother, Harry, who was also a pianist. To illustrate AABA form*, Harry asked Bill to play *Star Eyes* as simply as possible. It's kind of humorous, because Bill's simplest way of playing it was still very sophisticated, and would require working out and rehearsal by lesser pianists. It was clear that Bill Evans had imbibed his harmonic language so that he played with the same level of ease as others have in playing a simple melody. The tune came out of his hands the same way that the Scarlatti came out of Horowitz's hands.

---

*AABA = the form of most standard popular songs before Rock and Roll.

Another similarity with Horowitz occurred later in the video, when Harry asked Bill to improvise. This scene was really funny because in those days, Bill looked kind of like a nerd. You almost expected to see a bandaid on the bridge of his glasses, holding them together. When the camera showed his face, as with Horowitz, it looked as if he were just sitting there, not playing. When his hands were shown, they were grooving, playing the language they knew so well. Both artists exemplify the characteristics of effortless mastery.

Have Patience

Once while touring in Spain, I traveled to a beautiful seaside resort town. My room happened to face east with a beautiful view of the ocean. I decided to get up at dawn and do an open-eyed meditation so that I could witness all the stages of the sunrise. At first there was a subtle light that allowed a dim view of the cloud formations and the horizon. I could just make out the line where the ocean met the sky. It stayed like that for a long time: just a distant light signaling that the sun was in range. This light increased so slowly that I could not discern when one view gave way to another; it was liquid evolution. The change in colors and intensity was heralding the slow but unquestionable return of the sun for another day. Even in the later stages of illumination, the sky teased for a very long time, remaining in a fiery state, waiting for its lord. I could sense the absence of ego in all the elements.

The final stage was a hot yellow hue, the aura of father sun himself, with his closest attendants, the clouds, which were glowing from constant exposure to his magnificence. Finally, the lord of light cracked through. Just a sliver was visible, which increased in size at the same slow pace. I wondered if human beings could allow a composition to unfold like that.

For the seeker, this sunrise is a metaphor, to have patience with each stage before it evolves into the next. The sun rose in its own time. It may be slow, *but it always happens.*

Great patience and objectivity emanate from the inner space. You can see clearly what functions well and what doesn't. Also, from that space, you don't berate yourself for lapses in your playing. Without indulging in useless drama, you systematically chip away at your weak points. Longtime problems start to clear up, and you feel on track, perhaps for the first time. The thing is, *it's okay, no matter how long it takes.* If, in trying to move faster, you learn on mediocre levels, what can you expect? Mediocrity, of course.

Remember: barreling through material works for only a very few. The rest are clearly overwhelmed by that pace and fail to develop a relationship to the music, supporting the belief that they are not meant to play well, that they're not very talented. But by practicing small amounts, chewing fully and digesting everything from the lesson, extracting from it all the vitamins possible, one becomes mighty!

Summary

Mastery is comprised of two things:

1) *Staying out of the way and letting music play itself.*

I accept whatever wants to come out. I accept it *with love.* I accept the good and the bad with *equal love.* Without the drama of needing to sound good, I play from an effortless space. This takes deprogramming and reprogramming.

2) *Being able to play the material perfectly every time without thought.*

I practice thoroughly and patiently until *the material plays itself.* The ego no longer terrorizes me. When the material is properly digested, it comes out in an organic way and manifests as *my voice.*

Effortless technique, effortless language, total acceptance of what wants to come out: these are the components of the "master space."

Chapter 14
Meditation #2

(Please listen to Meditation #2 on CD)

*L*et yourself get comfortable. Relax, take a few deep breaths. Take another nice deep breath. A long deep breath is the cure for what ails us ... Begin to let your mind get quiet again. Each deep breath is like a wave that you can ride back into the ocean of the inner self. Breathe in ... nice and deep ... exhale ... long and slow ... and again ... let yourself get more and more relaxed. Let yourself get back to the place you reached in the first meditation. Once you design that place inside yourself, it becomes easier to go back there.

Your mind, as always, is filled with questions. Remember, you can have all your baggage back in a few minutes, but just for now, let go of all questions, all desires. You want to experience moments when you're not driven by these desires. Start to imagine what it feels like to play without these desires. Before you can do it while playing, you have to be able to do it *while just sitting.*

Let yourself rest in that comfortable, quiet space ... and imagine that you could do anything from that space. Imagine that you don't have to leave that space to function. See yourself playing your instrument from that effortless space.

Imagine yourself on the stage of Carnegie Hall. A blinding spotlight is on you. There are a hundred-thousand people in the audience. They're all looking at you, and *you're not doing anything but breathing!* You're sitting there and your hands, or lips, or whatever you use to make music, *are working by themselves.* You're sitting there just breathing, and your body is playing the instrument *without your participation. You're not involved.*

Now imagine that what's coming out *is the greatest music you've ever heard!* (This can be an enjoyable visualization.) Take another deep breath ... and go deeper into the world of your imagination. You're trying to imagine what mastery looks and feels like on you.

Again, you're on the stage of Carnegie Hall, and everyone is looking at you. But instead of feeling pressure, you're sitting in your chair or standing and just breathing. And your hands, feet, or lips are making the music for you. Something has taken you over ... and music is being played through you ... *while you rest!* ... Imagine that ...

You're beaming at the audience, and you're listening right along with them as it comes through you. Along with the audience, you're thinking, "Wow, this is great! *Who's playing this?*" ... The greatest music you've ever heard is coming out of you, and *you're not doing anything.* Imagine that. It's a fun fantasy. But, it is also the highest reality.

You have been receiving music out of a tiny opening for a long time. But now, imagine you are opening up to the ocean of music. Just see it. Get a taste. See it inside you. Taste the salt air of inspiration on your tongue. Imagine that the ocean is infinite sound. Every wave is a brilliant idea that pours through you, breaking down the sea walls of your mind. Imagine the dam bursting and you are drowning in the ecstasy of sound. Now imagine you died and became the ocean. You have no identity, no beginning, no end. You no longer play music. You *ARE* music ... Take a deep breath ... Now imagine yourself opening up to the infinite universe of sound, where music organizes itself through you in a unique way. Your music ... is just .... the music ... that comes through you. Not jazz ... your music ... not bebop ... your music. Music ... not American music ... *YOUR MUSIC*. It's coming from this ocean and you are drowning in it.

Take another deep breath and breathe in the water the way a fish does with his gills. Breathe in the thought, "I have no mind, I have no will, I have no control, I am the vessel, and music pours through me."

Take one more deep breath ...

Go deep inside now ... and see the ocean inside your heart. Call up your most profound memory of an ocean ... and see it in your own heart. Imagine that ocean is made of great, unlimited, brilliant ideas. See it inside you. Now imagine yourself opening up wide ... so wide that the ocean can pour through you. Imagine it pouring through you into and out of your instrument, and if you're a singer, imagine yourself singing wild, *amazing ideas!* ... You are like the mouth of a river: strong, silent and still, but channeling a never-ending current of ideas ... Again, give yourself this thought, *I am a master. I am great!* ... Don't tire of that thought. Give it to yourself again ... *I am a master. I am great* ...

You may say to yourself, "It's not working! I don't feel like a master. I don't feel great." Don't pay attention to that thought. That is just your mind *spoiling it again for you.* Keep saying it ... *I am a master* ... *I am great.*

If you would say that to yourself for the next ten years, your life would look very different from the way it looks today. Great things would come to you. You become your thoughts, so mastery would manifest in all aspects of your life. Every day you would be driving the thought in a little deeper through your whole being ... *I AM a master.*

More and more, the things you do would have mastery. More and more, the things you played would have mastery, but you must burn this thought into your consciousness and burn away all falsehoods. You must program yourself.

The thing that becomes true about you is the thing you think the most often.

If you think, "I am limited," that becomes true. If you think, "I am not too good," that becomes true. But if you think, "I *am God,*" that also becomes true. Whatever you think about yourself becomes a self-fulfilling prophecy. If you think, *"Every note I play is the most beautiful sound I've ever heard,"* that becomes true. Take a deep breath now, and inhale this concept.

Contemplate it ...

Right now, in this relaxed state, I am going to give you new thoughts of empowerment. Breathe deeply as you read them. Imagine each thought is on a boat, sailing out of the mouth of the river and into the ocean of your heart. Every thought ... put it on the boat ... sail it down the river ... through the mouth of the river ... and into the ocean.

Thought # 1:   *I am a master.* Send that down the river. *I am a master.* See it on the sailboat ... sailing off into the sunset. Imagine the sun is the center of your heart and the boat is sailing towards it. On the boat is the precious cargo: *I am a master.*

Thought #2:   *Music is easy.* Send that thought sailing peacefully down the river ... toward the sunset ... into the ocean. *Music is easy.*

Thought #3:   *I play music effortlessly.* Send that down.

Thought #4:   *I play music masterfully.*

Thought #5:   *Every note I play is the most beautiful sound I've ever heard.*

If you could program yourself into believing these things ... you would get a little crazy! ... Insane with joy ... insane ... with ecstasy ... enjoying every note you play ... laughing at the wrong notes ... loving them ... and making everyone believe ... *THAT THEY ARE THE NEW RIGHT NOTES!*

Don't worry if you're not feeling it at this moment ... *practice it for five years! ... ten years!* ... What do you have to lose?

Take another deep breath ... and return to the room.

Reprogramming

Think about it. Why should practicing this for ten minutes a day scare you? You waste more time than that every day. And you'll happily do that for the rest of your life. Why not borrow time from that hour or two a day that you waste and try saying these things deeply to yourself? Are you afraid it won't work? So what? You know the time you waste every day is going for naught. Why not try stealing ten minutes from that time to see if it can change the course of your life?

Chapter 15
Affirmations

Affirmations: Programming New Belief Systems

The experience of playing is colored by what you believe about music and what you believe about yourself. There are positive and negative belief systems. Positive belief systems can be the foundation for success and ease in your endeavors. Negative belief systems can inhibit success and growth. A belief system is not like an intellectual belief, which can be changed by proof to the contrary. Rather, it is a deeply-held and often subconscious belief about the way things are. As shown before, negative beliefs can be detrimental to your success. To change over time, those beliefs need consistent reprogramming. Affirmations are statements used for creating new, positive results.They can be valuable tools of reprogramming.

I've known great players who, no matter how much adulation they received worldwide, deluded themselves in the belief that they play badly, or in some way are not worthy of success. This shows that a belief system, positive or negative, often is not rooted in objective reality (something obvious to the rest of us). It is simply a program that feels comfortable. Even these gifted people may be holding themselves back from a greater career, higher mastery, and a richer life.

Affirmations are messages given over time. They may be true, but they don't have to be. I like to think of them as statements of truths yet unrealized. In this way, I can grow to accept the truth they contain. Affirmations can also be expressed in the form of visualization. You affirm a situation or a program change by "seeing yourself as that." You can literally see yourself in the situation you would like to create. For example, members of a broad jumping team were told to imagine that their arms and legs were ten feet long. They of course knew that this wasn't true, but by visualizing this image as clearly and realistically as possible, they were able to gain more extension and increase their performance. The sky is the limit on what you want to affirm or create. You don't have to temper your affirmation with what you think is "realistic." That is another trap, because what you think is realistic may well be tainted by a negative belief system. Affirmations given over time can change the program, create something you want, or change the patterns of your life so that you can bring about better results. You have to be patient, give the affirmation time to gestate, and, just as with practicing, detach from the results. Refrain from getting too emotionally involved in their manifestation.

I have used some phrases several times in the book to help with reprogramming. You might have already decided that they were fantasy. Let's contemplate their meaning and see if we can't find a way to accept them intellectually as being possibly true:

MUSIC IS EASY

Children start off life with this belief. If no one shoots them down, they may retain a positive outlook. I myself always believed, perhaps even arrogantly, that music was easy to do and nothing to worry about. If something is hard to play, my gut feeling is that I haven't seen the simplicity in it yet. That reflects my instinctual belief that *all music is easy.*

THERE ARE NO WRONG NOTES

As stated before, this affirmation can free you as an improviser, and if you use it as an interpreter of classical music, you will develop a sure hand. Notes that were not regarded as usable in one time period were used freely in the next, thereby proving that their wrongness only existed in the mind. *Human beings make up this stuff!* There are not, and never have been, any wrong notes. If you live near the ocean, you may hear a seagull squawking in one key, a dog barking in another key, the roar of the ocean out of tune with the other two sounds, and birds singing in clashing rhythms with all of these, and you'll say, "Beautiful!" But if human beings pick up instruments and do the same thing, the average listener won't be able to stand it! Why? Because his mind says, "This is supposed to be music." The very concept of music is superimposed by humans. Beneath this concept lies the greater reality of sound, and beneath that, the fabric of the entire universe, vibration. It is vibration that makes music; it is vibration that makes matter, including our bodies. *We are vibration,* therefore, it may be said that *we are music.* So vibration is the raw clay. With our minds, we mold it into whatever we want. We may have created a social and moral structure through a thing called music, but the truth is that *any sound goes with any sound.* That can be as troubling to the human mind, with its craving for order, as accepting chaos as a natural state.

We are programmed to believe in a certain order of things musically. Why destroy that programming? *Because that order is confining our spirits.* Too much sensitivity to the rightness and wrongness of what we're doing makes us tentative and clumsy, releasing uncertainty in the air that robs even the right notes of their power. As I stated earlier, *a note is only as powerful as the player believes it to be.* If the musician has evolved to embrace the belief that there are no wrong notes, then he can play all the wrong notes, and they'll sound right.

One way to practice this is to sit at a piano and play different intervals. Meditate on them as you play them slowly and quietly over and over. Contemplate their sound without forming any opinions. Try to resist all previous attitudes toward the sound and just ... *listen.* The sound will become more and more consonant, more friendly, more personal. Your relationship to it will go through many levels until it is yours. It will be inside you. About the only sound in the twelve tone system that still has any illusion of dissonance is the flat 9 interval, a half-step wider than an octave, generally considered to be a "clashing" sound. So I guess that would be a good place to start. Make that clash the sweetest sound in your mind. Form a personal relationship to every interval, every chord, indeed to every sound in the universe. Consonance is simply a *harmonious relationship with a sound.*

A good analogy is the fear we feel towards certain ethnic or socioeconomic groups. We view people who are different with discomfort and distrust. Usually, a personal experience over time with people of different backgrounds wipes away preconceptions and helps us view them as individuals worthy of love and respect. When we transcend such barriers, we feel liberated. It is the same when you transcend musical barriers. You feel as if you are breathing rarefied air, and it's exhilarating.

You may further cleanse your mind of negativity by using this affirmation:

EVERY NOTE I PLAY IS THE MOST BEAUTIFUL SOUND I'VE EVER HEARD.

Examine this statement. At first, it seems absurd. But it has the power to create profound inroads to freedom. Who's to say what is beautiful? Isn't that programming, just like everything else? Haven't the fashion and advertising industries brainwashed us to believe that "bony is beautiful"? Right now, you are programmed to view and hear beauty in a very narrow frequency. The music you hear beyond a limited range seems chaotic. Without preconceptions, you could handle and enjoy much more chaos in music.

In a movie, you might have heard the most dissonant music ever played, but if someone were having their throat cut on the screen, your ears would accept it. Perhaps the dead psychopath on the floor wasn't really dead! As he lunged one more time for the girl's ankles, you might have heard the most frightening sound an orchestra can make — Witold Lutoslowski's worst nightmare. With your eyes stimulated by that visual, the ear canals relax and dilate, and you can handle that sound.

If you drop your two hands heavily on the piano and let it ring, you might not be programmed to regard that as the most beautiful sound you ever heard, but what if you hit your refrigerator or stove and it made the same sound? You'd stand there all day like a fool beating your refrigerator, or you'd invite your friends over to hear your stove!

Don't forget: music is something we just made up. It doesn't actually exist as anything but a game for us, so how did we get trapped in our own game? By imposing values on it.

Spiritually speaking, is this not considered the enlightened point of view? The Jewish scriptures teach us to regard all men as brothers: to "love thy neighbor as thyself." In Hinduism and other Eastern paths, we are told to see God in ourselves and in each other. Certain Buddhist sects are not allowed to harm even an insect, believing that all things are equally sacred. When, through practice, one adapts that awareness, one exists in heaven while on earth, intoxicated by beauty all around and filled with compassion for all things great and small.

The thing to realize is that everything we think now, every opinion we have about everything – is the result of some kind of programming. We do not possess absolute objectivity. Scientists have been similarly humbled. In the world of physics, they've arrived at the conclusion that they really can't observe anything with total objectivity because, as they shed light on it for the purposes of observation, the light changes its composition. This is known as the "uncertainty principle." All of this shows us that what we think, see, and hear is subjective. Therefore, it might behoove us to adopt the beliefs from which we get the most mileage. Believing that every sound is beautiful will open the way for more inspired playing. Become the Will Rogers of music by saying, "I never met a note I didn't like."

Chapter 16

The Steps To Change

$\mathcal{A}$ meaningful path is a path of action. The goal is achieved through practice. Without practices, a path is mere philosophy. Be careful of that. A philosophy is thought about and talked about, but a path is for walking. A good path is reduced to mere philosophy because one has not done the work to attain its fruits — like the alcoholic who can speak eloquently about how to stop drinking, but can't actually do it. Many people *talk the talk,* but don't *walk the walk.* No significant changes occur without practice. Talk is cheap, and in fact may be harmful to growth, because as you talk about the path, you may dissipate its power to change you. You also risk freezing the experience so that you won't be able to recognize the spontaneous way wisdom wants to manifest today. As surely as one practices an instrument, so must one practice the implementation of wisdom.

There are many books and practices that help one attain the "space." As I once heard a wise man say, "There are many boats." However, the exercises I'm about to describe, which I call "steps," are relevant to the execution of music. They will help you develop focus, efficiency and fearlessness, and help you make the inner connection. Remember: you can be aware of all the philosophy and still be unable to attain its fruits while playing. The following steps will help you to let go and improve. You can experience functionality and follow a consistent game plan. Mental health is restored as you learn to stay in the moment. You may even eliminate those endless hours obsessing about your life.

We have talked a lot about the impurities of your purpose, your playing, and your practicing. Now we are going to look at a method of deprogramming and reprogramming. There are four steps in making this change in your life.

Step One introduces you to the inner self. It is a kind of meditation, a sharp contrast to the space people usually play in. As previously stated, many have experienced this state from activities like riding a bicycle, running or swimming, meditating and chanting, various martial arts and ancient tea ceremonies. Zen and yogic traditions are drenched in the awareness of this space. I've met musicians who have studied other disciplines and have attained the fruits of those disciplines, but could not retain the awareness while playing. It is just a matter of *touching the instrument in that state,* but they could never do that because they missed one little point: ***you must surrender the need to sound good. Otherwise, you can't really let go!*** Simple, but not easy! Learn a way of attaining inner balance and approach your instrument while in that space. The first two steps will help you observe all the thoughts and pressures connected with your instrument. You will learn to let go and love whatever you hear coming out. This is absolutely necessary to escape your dilemma. You can't fake it! Step One will help you get in touch with your intuitive self by bypassing the conscious mind, the epitome of all limited playing. Physically, you will intuitively move towards the most effortless and efficient way of playing your particular instrument. Daily practice will allow you to become familiar with the more effortless stance, or perfect embouchure, head position, or whatever. You will gravitate to the physical position that allows you to play *without leaving the space.*

Step Two is the retention of that awareness while the hands explore the instrument in a free improvisation. I don't mean the style of free jazz, but the intent. Your hands are free to wander, *without your conscious participation.* Again, this is only possible if you can release the need to sound good for a few moments.

If Steps One and Two are analogous to crawling, Step Three is beginning to walk. In Step Three you will learn how to do simple things from this consciousness. The natural space you developed forms a foundation from which you relearn how to play. In this step, music begins to play through you in intelligent form. You start to experience what wants to be played, and what *you can comfortably play.* You learn to stay within yourself and not be seduced by your ego. Just as the space established your natural connection to your instrument and sound, it now establishes what can be played effortlessly over form, time, changes, written music or whatever. It will be humbling to discover your true level of play. But it will also be the start of becoming real, and your playing will be built on more solid ground. Leaving the ego out of the playing will remove the drama of trying to play what *you wish you could play*. You will be practicing the wisdom of accepting, with love, *what you can play from the space*.

The space itself is the teacher, and life becomes centered around learning to connect with the space. Music becomes secondary. You remember gigs not by how well you played, but by how much you let go. Those are usually the best gigs anyway, but now the priority has changed. You're no longer bothered by what is out there, but absorbed by *what is in here*.

You are not condemned to your present level of playing for life, however, because in Step Four you begin a process of change and growth. Built on the solid foundation of the first three steps, with detachment and calm, and with self-love, you begin practicing things that can't be played effortlessly. Not only do you practice from the space, but you don't assume you've mastered anything until *it plays itself from that space*. Step Four will help you acquire a taste for absorption into a subject, rather than skimming uselessly over many subjects. The discipline of patience overtakes you as you wait in a detached way for *mastery to occur* on what you are practicing. Every practice session becomes a link in a chain, a patient process that moves you toward your goal.

These steps can be life-transforming. You'll feel as free as a bird when you play, yet have great discipline in all your studies. If patiently followed, these four steps will transform your practice and performance.

Chapter 17

Step One

$\mathcal{W}$e will describe several ways of doing step one, depending on what instrument you play. Each method calls for a complete relaxation of the body. To begin this step, you could use meditation 1, the "I am a master" meditation. If you start the day with that meditation, you will learn to easily slip into this space. Take a very deep breath and blow out a very long, slow breath. Relax every muscle from the top of your head ... your forehead ... back of the head ... ears ... eyes ... nose ... cheeks ... mouth ... tongue ... throat ... neck ... shoulders ... shoulder blades ... upper back ... chest ... spine ... rib cage ... heart ... lungs ... kidneys ... lower back ... stomach ... upper arms ...   elbows ... forearms ...wrists ... hands and fingers.

Take another deep breath and relax your hips ... buttocks ... thighs ... knees ... calves ... ankles and feet.

It is very important to let your mind go as much as you're willing to ... Let go of all thoughts as you breath deeply ... let go of music ... just for a few moments ... and now ... let go of the need to be a great player ... If you find you can't do it ... then just pretend for now ... See the possibilities of freedom ... as if you just didn't ... care!

Now you might feel your body and mind letting go. Inside, there may be a feeling of stillness, focus and inner connection. If you can't quiet your mind, then just try to observe your thoughts. Watch them come and go as if they weren't yours. You will find that with practice, you will slip into a steady space where you feel quite empty. As you enjoy this space, begin to feel as if you're not in control of your body. Imagine that you are like a puppet and someone is moving your muscles.

If you're relaxed, your body will naturally adjust to the most comfortable position. Your belly might drop as you are relaxing the muscles there. Deep breathing is priceless, and you can learn to drop into this space simply from a deep exhalation, like a sigh.

Assuming you've relaxed yourself through meditation, or by the instructions in this chapter, we will go through step one on a few different instruments:

Piano

Sit in a comfortable position and relax all parts of your body. Let your spine feel elongated, as if it were hanging from an iron pole that is connected directly to the ceiling. In this way, your back is straight. Imagine that the pole is holding you up; you don't have to force yourself to sit straight. Let your arms rest in your lap or hang at your sides.

Now imagine that someone or something is lifting your arm, right or left, and floating it over to the keyboard. Try to imagine as much as possible that *someone else is doing this for you.* Let your hand float up over the keyboard and settle down slowly until the fingertips touch the white keys. Imagine that your arm is filled with helium or is as light as a feather, and that the fingertips touching the keys are enough to keep the arm hovering in mid-air. The arm should be about level with the keyboard. Even though you are relaxed, you shouldn't let the arm hang down with the fingers holding on. The arm should feel as if it is floating in the air, level with the keyboard, while the fingertips "lightly kiss" the white keys. Again, the best result occurs if you imagine someone else is doing this for you while *you are resting.*

Now focus your mind on your thumb, the first finger ... Imagine you are sending your consciousness down into that finger ... Imagine someone is lifting the thumb just a little ... The thumb should be lifted only as high as *it wants to go.* There should be no sense of stretch or strain. At first, you may feel that the fingers hardly want to move. They are so used to being forced to move by you. Now to whatever extent the thumb is willing to move, let it do so. It might be helpful to breath in slowly as you raise the thumb and hold it up for a moment, while staying as conscious as you can (staying in the space). Then just drop the finger onto the key ... It may hardly move the key, but that doesn't matter. Just drop it and exhale with the dropping ... You might also imagine your finger sinking into the key as a means of depressing it, but refrain from using force of any kind. You are learning the effortlessness of movement, the Zen-like technique of a finger dropping by itself, while you observe.

Next, apply this awareness to the second finger, imagining your consciousness to be contained in that little finger ... Then, with as much focus and attention as possible, watch as the second finger is lifted for you, as high as it wants to go ... Inhale as you do this, then hold it there for a few moments, making sure that you have not left your center; then drop or sink the finger into that key while you exhale ... Repeat the same actions with the third finger ... and so on ...

Before lifting, be sure to take the time to focus your attention on each finger. You will actually be practicing great levels of awareness and focus. This alone will affect your playing in ways you can't imagine. You'll feel this focus creep into your playing over time. The trick is to give it time.

Repeat the process with each finger. Thumb to fifth finger, then fifth finger to thumb. After you finish one hand, if you still have the patience and concentration for it, you may start the other hand. Begin the whole process again, but if you are short of the patience, awareness or stillness necessary for this exercise, then please STOP! It would be better to do only two fingers completely from the space than all the fingers from a compromised space. You can always break up the exercise into little two-to-five-minute practices in your day. That way you can avoid frustration or burn-out from such concentration.

It may seem like a heavy or difficult thing you're doing, but it is not. *Keep it light.* Treat it as a moment to relax and tune in gently to your inner self while touching the piano. You may actually feel invigorated from these little moments.

Horn Players

Sit in a comfortable chair and start to relax ... Do one of the meditations or anything you know to gently descend into the space ... Have the horn sitting nearby on a chair, a stand or on the floor ... Now surrender control of your body completely ... Imagine that someone is using your body like one would use a puppet ... He or she is moving your arm and reaching over to pick up the horn. Remember to pretend that it's not you. This will result in a feeling of effortlessness and detachment. Now go back to the previous position with your horn in hand and let it rest on your lap ... You will notice that whatever calm you were able to achieve has been stirred by just holding the horn. There will be a definite increase in mental activity and overall agitation. This is because you have so many old messages as to what it means to touch your horn. It might be a totally new experience to just *hold it with no desire.* You've learned to think, to try, and even to obsess from the moment you touch it. Previously programmed thoughts emerge every time to stir up your mind. But now ... *let everything quiet down* ... Breathe deeply while holding the horn in your lap ... It will begin to feel different than ever before ... Pretend it is just a piece of metal. Let your fingers and hands notice things about it. Is it rough or smooth? Is it cold or hot? Noticing these general things will take you further from the idea that it's your horn, and hence further away from the obsession. When you've completely returned to that quiet space, you're ready to move forward ... Take this very slowly, because you are likely to lose this space the closer you get to playing, so you must be careful to keep returning to it between every move. This absolute consciousness will pay off in a big way later on. You will eventually retain this state throughout every phase of practice and play. That is why it is extremely important to experience it fully from the beginning.

Now you are ready to bring the horn to your mouth. No matter how you like to play the horn, for this exercise, *let the horn come to your mouth; don't move your head towards the mouthpiece.*

Note to Saxophonists:

I've worked with a number of saxophone players, and we almost always find that the strap has not been placed in the most natural position for air to move through the horn. The strap is usually too low, forcing the saxophonist to reach down with his neck, much like an ostrich. This causes him to lose the "space" before getting the horn to his lips. In its most natural position, the neck is usually elongated. In addition, the spine tends to be straight and the upper torso balances on the hips. You should find that position and simply *add the horn to that posture, wherever your head is.* When you do so, the horn suddenly becomes easier to blow, and your face and neck relax. Even if you don't choose to play this way, try this posture when practicing the first step. Air moves through the horn with greater ease if you don't cut it off at the neck. It will help establish an effortless connection and the feeling that *someone is playing you playing the horn.*

Bring the horn to your mouth and, again, pause ... As you bring the horn to your lips, your mind will again become active with petty considerations, and the space will be lost. You simply have to hold the horn in your mouth – or, in the case of brass players, against your lips – take a deep breath, and again let go of all thoughts. You will feel something new. You can feel the mouthpiece on a sensory level. Is it rough or smooth? Cool or warm? Eventually you will sink into a oneness with the mouthpiece, not really noticing where your mouth ends and the mouthpiece begins. You will feel more connected to the horn than ever before. Then it will be time to stir the mind once again with the thought of *playing it!*

Take your deepest breath and hold it as long as you can. Imagine that someone else is using your lungs to take the breath.

Every time you do that, it will have the effect of relaxing every other part of you, while only the muscles needed will be used. It will also reinforce the notion that *someone is doing this for you.* That notion can have profound spiritual implications. So take that breath and hold it, and when you can't hold it any longer, release it through the mouthpiece. *Don't attempt to control the sound at all!* Let it be as ugly as it wants to be!

After that one note, rest the horn in your lap again and *go back into the space.* You'll find that the act of playing has stirred the mind yet again. What we are trying to learn is how to play and practice without leaving the space. How will you ever do that if you can't even stay there through one note? Step One is about learning how to move from within the space.

Rest the horn on your lap, take a deep breath and *let go of the previous experience.* Don't think about it, evaluate it or even remember it. Just return to as quiet and focused a place as possible ...

When you've quieted down again, imagine that someone is again bringing the horn to your mouth. Hold it there and breathe to release any thoughts or agitation. From that still state, take a breath, not so deep this time, and blow through the horn while accepting whatever sound comes out without conscious control or evaluation. You are building consciousness. You are practicing getting to and remaining in an ancient state of inner wisdom that is not compromised by the desire to play well.

In the beginning, it is better to play one note and then put the horn down. You are not trying to play. You are just trying to stay detached, to stay in the space while playing anything. Repeat this a few times and put the horn down. That is the end of step one.

Vocalists

Stand straight and balance yourself well on the balls of your feet. Then let your feet root themselves into the ground (the mountain pose, a yogic posture, might be very helpful). Do the relaxation technique of your choice, and close your eyes ... Begin to take a slow, deep breath and imagine that someone else is doing it for you ... Feel your chest swell and your lungs slowly inflate ... When you can't inhale any longer, hold your breath ... Hold it and feel the pressure to release it build. While you are holding it, imagine that you have no control of your voice once you exhale ... Imagine that the exhalation is going to be sung ... Finally, let go of the breath and let the force of the exhalation release a note into the air. Stay focused on your center while the note sings itself. Imagine that it is not your voice. As you hear the sound (it may be loud or soft), don't be afraid of its crudeness or force. That sound contains the seeds of your true voice, not the one you've been "stylizing" for "correctness."

Relax after that note ... It can be a traumatic experience for some ... Let your breathing be regular and easy for a few moments. If you left the space (which you probably have), take a moment to bring yourself back into the space. The idea concerning your instrument, as it is with all others, is to let the note come from that space. Let it bypass all the fear and feeling of inadequacy that is so typical of singers, especially in jazz. Jazz singers often don't feel appreciated by other jazz musicians. Rather than honor themselves for the special thing they can do that the others can't, they often lose self-respect in the classroom while trying to learn theory, harmony or scat singing. They feel invalid unless they can do what the instrumentalists can do, when the truth is that they have an instrument that the other musicians cannot come close to: the voice. And they also have the added dimension of words with which they can communicate. In the old days, instrumentalists had more respect for the power of the singer; but today, they are so preoccupied with their next solo that they don't have any interest in vocalists. They lay head trips on the vocalists and imply that they are inferior for not being able to solo. The vocalists internalize this negativity, besides any that they had received as children, and the result is a lot of singers who don't have any confidence. A singer with that mind-set sings with such timidity that there is nothing compelling to listen to. *That singer cannot commit to the sound of his or her own voice. Hence the fear ...*

So let's gear up for that next deep breath. And this time, let go of some of that fear, and loathing, and, perhaps anger, and hitch a ride on this next note! Keep doing the exercise until the note is freely escaping your control. React to it with unqualified joy and acceptance, and resist any urge to judge it. And be assured: that urge will come. Resisting it is like trying not to scratch an itch!

For any instrument, practice letting go and getting relaxed while touching your instrument. Over time, these exercises will have the residual effect of reversing your attachment to your performance, and *you will become light and relaxed!* All problems will fade as you merge with the instrument. For many of you, it is presently the other way around. You may be relatively calm, but anxiety rises within you because *it's time to play!*

Summing Up

These practices and contemplations have taken me to a nice place. No matter what head space I'm in (and believe me, I get into some strange ones), when I touch the piano, I go into a space where everything is beautiful. There is no sin, no wrong notes, all there is is love and joy (and usually a lot of laughs.) I wish I could have a piano strapped around my neck at all times. I might even become sane! Mildred Chase speaks about this state of mind in her book, *Just Being At The Piano*: "*It is impossible to be self-conscious and totally involved in the music at the same time. Consciousness of the self is a barrier between the player and the instrument. As I forget my own presence, I attain a state of oneness with the activity and become absorbed in a way that defies the passage of time.*"[1] If you program effortlessness into your connection with your instrument, the result will be that when you play, *you will drop into that space.* You will slip into your most open, effective and concentrated space by playing. Instead of it being an instrument of torture,

---

[1]Chase, Mildred. *Just Being at the Piano.* Berkeley: Creative Arts Books.

as it is for many, it will be an instrument of ecstasy! Playing will become as natural as breathing. Many people I've worked with have immediately felt from this letting go that their instrument was easier to play than they ever thought! How important is that? As I stated before, the easier it is to physically play the instrument, the more you will be able to play, and the freer you will feel. If you have an exercise that reminds you daily how easy it is to play, you will see dramatic improvement from that alone. From the concert stage to the sports arena, the people who really excel are those for whom the activity is easier than for others. For some, it is so easy! When I began this process myself, all I had was this first step. It was enough to change my playing and, eventually, my life.

I like to say that the most comfortable seat in my house — psychically, physically, mentally and otherwise – is the piano seat. After some years of letting your inner self take over, you will feel that same relationship with your instrument. Step One is a focusing of the mind and a release of the spirit from prison. Start to unlock that spirit now.

Chapter 18

Step Two

"The Way [The Great Tao] is not difficult, just avoid picking and choosing."

Seng-Tsan[1]

After practicing Step One for a while, you will have become comfortable going into the space and touching your instrument. Now comes the time to turn the heat up a bit. Although you have learned how to free yourself from attachment when playing one note, can you stay detached while moving around the instrument? How long before your mind takes the bait and starts trying to make musical sense? How long before you start "picking and choosing"? You need to be able to play freely on the instrument without consequences. Stephen Nachmanavich makes this point eloquently: "There is a time to do just anything, to experiment without fear of consequences, to have a play space safe from fear of criticism, so that we can bring out our unconscious material without censoring it."[2] In Step Two, we can practice flying without worrying about flight patterns.

Simply allow your hands to make random choices. Whether it be free improvisation, the repetition of one chord, or the simplest diatonic melody, those choices will be made from your hands, lips or vocal chords – but not from your head. There will be no intentionality to them. Rather, it will be as if you are asleep, but your hands are moving around the instrument. Or you could imagine your hands having their own consciousness and running

---

[1]Seng-Tsan. *Hsin Hsin Meng*. [eighth century]. Translated by D.T. Suzuki in *Essays in Zen Buddhism*. London: Rider, 1951.
[2]Nachmanovich, Stephen. *Free Play*, Los Angeles: Jeremy P. Tarcher, Inc., 1990. (p. 69).

the show while you observe. If you are singing, you could let your voice wander without worrying about pitch or tone. With horn players, it would be a matter of letting your hands and embouchure do what they want to do. Drummers could imagine their arms waving around and bumping into drums and cymbals. On the piano, I sometimes imagine that my hands are little animals grazing the pastures of the keyboard, or little mice running up and down. While they are doing their thing, I am *just watching.* That's the point: you aren't involved. You are only an observer.

This step develops the ability to detach from controlled playing so that creation may manifest itself, using you as the vehicle, yet unimpeded by you. Step Two allows you to appreciate what's coming out as if you were the listener, not the player. As I've stated many times, this level of consciousness is the goal. It is the true goal of art and music disciplines. In *Zen In The Art Of Archery*, the master explains to his student the value of detachment: "The right art — is purposeless, aimless! The more obstinately you try to learn how to shoot the arrow for the sake of hitting the goal, the less you will succeed in the one, and the further the other will recede. What stands in your way is that you have a much too willful will. You think that what you do not do yourself does not happen."[3] Isn't that our experience in music? The more we try to play, the more the play eludes us. This "purposelessness" and "aimlessness" can be practiced right here in Step Two. It is a means of establishing ourselves as the channel. Just let your hands move, slowly or quickly.

You can see that some of the fruits of the first step are already required here:

1. the ability to detach and observe;

2. imagining that your body is working by itself while you rest in the space;

3. the space itself.

---

[3]Eugen Herrigel, *Zen In The Art Of Archery* p. 31

There are absolutely no requirements with regard to tempo, key, or anything else. All you do is to allow whatever *wants to happen*. It is not as easy as it sounds, however, for as soon as your hands start to move, you'll feel your mind on the move again. Because of all its previous programming, the mind will try to lure you into "picking and choosing," in its programmatic search for "acceptable music." When the mind does this, *take your hands off the instrument!* In the case of portable instruments, *put them down*. Release the instrument and go back to the space ... Take a deep breath and just settle back into the stillness of non-doership ... Get out of the swirl of the hurricane and back into the eye ... where everything is peaceful ... Detach ...

In other words, re-apply the fruits of Step One.

Every time you move off the instrument and return to the space, you will bring more of the space back to the instrument.

In all the steps, and in all forms of practice, one should *remove one's hands from the instrument often*. I can't stress this strongly enough. That is the only way to go back to the space, or to find out if you've left the space. You need to step back and regain a perspective. The periodic act of releasing the instrument from your grasp also sends a message of detachment. Remember: *you don't need this instrument!* Paradoxically, the more you feel as though you can walk away at any time, *the more powerful your playing becomes!* This is the essence of Step Two. Moving around the instrument without trying, without caring. Your feeling for sound and touch will be revitalized.

We have to re-program the urge to control. We are so used to analyzing everything that we play in narrow, unforgiving terms. Some people think that this is dedication and humility, but it is just plain inhibition. There is a very positive way to analyze what you play, which will be discussed in the third step. But for now, let me just say that *analysis should not come during the playing, but well after the whole experience is over.* Music should occur totally devoid of thought. Nachmanavich says, "Fear of failure, and frustration; these are society's defenses against creativity."[4] I say, *"It is better to make bad music from a liberated state than to make reasonably good music from a state of bondage."*

STEP 2A The Monk Principle

We must block out the self-judging voice in our head with absolute faith. I call this Step 2A, because it still involves the unrestrained playing of notes by the hands. But it is all really part of the second step. You drop your hands anywhere on the piano, or anywhere on the drums, or play any note on any instrument; and before the mind has a chance to evaluate it, you say to yourself, *"That is the most beautiful sound I've ever heard."* This is the positive brainwashing I was talking about earlier. If you can hear your notes as beautiful, they will *be beautiful. Even the ugly ones!* I call this the Monk Principle, because I believe this to be Monk's great secret power. He enjoyed exploring the realm of the incorrect, and his inner acceptance convinced us all. I think the reason he quit playing could have been that he couldn't find any more wrong notes to play!

When you say to yourself, *"That is the most beautiful sound I've ever heard,"* make sure you don't get the words *that* and *is* turned around to say *"Is that the most beautiful sound?"* Before you have a chance to evaluate it, say *that is* ... Now do that for eight hours! Play notes with the abandon of a fool!

Step 2B

Imagine you could step out of your body and see the back of your head ... Then step back again and see the back of both heads ... Then step out out of that head ... and watch the hair in the back of that head ... then again, watch the back of that head. Keep doing this until you see a row of heads in front of you ... It will feel as though you are sending your consciousness to the

---

[4]Nachmanovich, Stephen. *Free Play*, Los Angeles: Jeremy P. Tarcher, Inc., 1990. (p. 138).

back of the room ... This is an old technique for slipping into meditation. Your mind will get quiet, and you might feel a bit high. You will also find that you are not able to control your playing from that state. With your mind way behind your body, put your hands on the instrument. Your hands have no choice but to move freely and independently. You will then hear and receive the sound with the thought, *"That is the most beautiful sound."*

Step 2C: *Playing Fast*

Some people feel that they can never play fast because their fingers are not exercised enough. I was once reading about a certain method for finger technique, and although I did not agree with all of it, I did read one thing that was very interesting. A study was done in which the finger speed of a well-trained concert pianist was measured against that of a non-pianist. He found that there wasn't much difference between two. What slows the fingers down is being unsure of where to drop them. After years of study and playing, a pianist may be so constricted that he cannot let go and experience the finger speed of a non-pianist! For that reason, this exercise can be very therapeutic, both physically and psychologically.

Go into the space (by now, you know what that means), let your arms approach the instrument, and then with no thought to right or wrong notes, just move your fingers as fast as possible. Wiggle them over the keys! If you are a horn player, take the deepest breath, hold it as long as possible, and release it into the horn while you move your fingers as fast as possible over the keys. You will be surprised at how truly fast you are, and it will liberate your technique for more specific playing later. You'll feel fluidity, and you'll know what fast playing should feel like!

2D Mimic Playing

Some will always find it hard not to react to what they are hearing. For this reason, it is very liberating to play in the air. A horn player should imagine that the horn is in the hands and just freely play it. Don't be concerned with what you are playing, or the actual correctness of playing the horn. Just mimic the act of playing that instrument in the air, the general feeling of wiggling your fingers and blowing. In this way without being hooked into what you're hearing, you will experience the freedom of movement that you are looking for with the horn in your hands! If you play piano, let your hands float in the air while your arms move from side to side and your fingers wiggle, either quickly or slowly. One good thing about this is that it can be practiced anywhere, even on the subway! You begin to feel unbelievably free. I say *unbelievably* because, due to old belief systems, you'll probably have trouble believing it! This is what it feels like to play fast with a free spirit.

Now we will mold this freedom into form.

Chapter 19

Step Three

$\mathcal{N}$ow we can touch our instrument with complete abandon. We can let our hands roam, blissfully unaware of their destination, and we can proclaim anything that we hear come out as ultimately beautiful. Now what? It's time to play!

Oh no! Not that. How on earth can I keep this space if I have to obey a tempo, key area, or – even worse – chord changes? This is truly a dilemma!

Remember the fear of giving up control that we addressed in Steps One and Two? That fear asserts itself anew when trying Step Three. Don't we need to control ourselves to play in time and in form? No, not if time and form are as comfortable as the timeless and formless. When classical performers play, don't they need to retain some rigidity to execute all the parameters of the piece? No, not in a piece well learned. As stated before, nothing in music is hard, just unfamiliar. Once you are familiar with something, it is no longer difficult. This is where Step Three can be humbling. Remember that mastery was defined as the perfect, effortless execution of whatever you are playing. Whatever you know on that level will manifest when you play from the space. *The humbling part is finding out how little you really do know from there.*

Believe it or not, this is really good news. It finally explains the difference between you and the masters. It isn't race, religion, size, shape or even talent. It is how deeply the material is known. Step Three exposes all the glitches and gremlins in your knowledge that have been sabotaging your playing. The technical reasons for why you don't swing or burn, for why you lack fluidity or cannot create on the level of your desires are exposed to you. Consider this equation: ***The effort it takes for you to perform music equals the distance between you and mastery.***

For example, if you play a tune from this space, you will notice that you play some parts perfectly. Perhaps you are occasionally playing the right changes, or the melody comes out correctly from time to time. Check to see if those aren't the places in the tune where you also improvise best.

Our ability to shine is very much dependent on our familiarity with the material. This holds true in absorbing a classical piece. But, because of the shoddy way we have practiced in the past, our game is full of holes, full of things that we don't know as well as we thought we did.

Step Three is get-real time. It is a soul-searching inventory of what we have learned and what we haven't: of what we own and what we *think is ours.* This inventory should be taken as dispassionately as if checking on our supply of groceries or toilet paper. We just want to find out what works and what doesn't, and design our practicing accordingly. This is why we have been cultivating detachment in the previous steps. We need to detach so that we can be honest without becoming depressed.

For improvisers, this step is also about honest expression, the stripping down of our playing to only that which wants to be expressed – not that which the ego strives for. Ego usually leads us beyond our capabilities of the moment, creating sloppy, overplayed music. When one dwells in that "still small place inside," observing from a detached place, the music that emanates is essential, creating great depth of expression. This is the illusive quality of the true masters that I talked about earlier. Surrendering to the "inner notes" could be called the Miles Principle, for that was his gift and his magic.

In Step Two, you had to learn not to interfere, but to observe. The process here is the same: get into the space employing any method you've found to get there, such as the meditations in this book, and do Step One. (That should be a daily practice.) Decide in advance what specific piece or improvisation you are going to play. Then imagine someone lifting your hands to the instrument. Then, simply start to play. Don't try to play the piece in time or out of time. Don't try to play the right changes or notes, but instead see which ones come out correctly. If the only thing that wants to come is the melody, do just that. If it's simple changes or voicings way beneath your taste or the most un-clever playing you've ever done, *just go with it.* Don't embellish what's happening; just observe from a detached place. As soon as you get seduced into trying to play, STOP. *Stop and go back to the space.* That is the most important part. You must stop, no matter how much your ego is screaming at you to *save this solo*; just stop and put down the instrument! Once you've returned to the space, you may go back to the instrument and do it again. You may start from the place you stopped, or at the beginning. Bring your playing back into the space as if you were towing a ship into the harbor. If you're playing a classical piece, put your hands on the instrument from the space, and just start playing it without caution. The mistakes that result are fine, and, as with the improviser, as soon as your detachment erodes and you can feel yourself tensing to perform the piece correctly, stop, return to the space, and with trust embark upon the piece again. When playing the piece from the space, sacrifice the tempo rather than the correct notes. In that case, let your hands float over the notes of the piece effortlessly while you remain in a semi-meditative state. This is a very powerful way of programming your hands to know the piece without your conscious control. Later, you can just let the piece fly and you might be amazed at *how much your hands have remembered by themselves!*

Now, you might only play a couple of bars, either written or improvised, before the mind jumps in. In fact, you might not play more than a couple of notes. It doesn't matter. *You must stop right there, take a deep breath, and then resume.* It is very difficult to catch the moment when your mind has jumped in. Having tried to make music for so many years, you're not even sure what "not trying" feels like. That is why it is so important to learn the first two steps very thoroughly, so that you have firm connection to the space. Then, if you can keep from caring too much about the sounds you're making, you have a chance to succeed. You have to *stay focused on the space and not on the playing.* This is best accomplished with the help of an auditor. But for now, let's try to describe the necessary attributes for you to begin practicing alone.

As I said, it will be absolutely necessary to have created, built, and strengthened your sense of surrender through the first step, your connection to the space, and your ability to let your hands move without your interference. Then, treat the playing in Step Three as if it were a fact-finding mission. You could tape record your playing and take note of everything that didn't work. These are the things that you would begin to work on in the fourth step. Don't worry if some of your problems are very basic. It is actually a boon to find the basic flaws that are holding you back. You are not used to playing without control, so it is much like a baby learning to crawl.

As I said before, the first time you approach Step Three, you may do remarkably little; perhaps after the first bar of a tune, you will already start trying. As painful as this might be, you have to stop and practice letting the first bar play itself. For example, if you are playing the standard composition *Stella By Starlight,* after you play E-7b5 (the first chord of *Stella*), you may have to think about where A7 b13 (the second chord of *Stella*) is. If that is so, just practice moving your hands from the E-7b5 to the A7b13 without thinking. You'll notice a feeling of sure-handedness that you've never felt, a feeling that your hands are playing those two chords by themselves. You will want to expand the things you can play like that.

If you grow to the point where you can play a simple melody with all the chord changes from that space, that will be a great start. Then see if you can keep time, or if any improvisation on the changes wants to happen or not. If you still find that you can't be rhythmic, that you lose the time, or that you can't find the right notes over the changes, these are the "unfamiliar things" that you can deal with in Step Four. The classical musician will find the execution of simple passages on that level very seductive and liberating. As technique *asserts itself,* the player is *free to feel something while playing!* He or she will be motivated to find that level of ease in more demanding passages.

Another Way of Doing Step Three

Although many musicians are used to playing in a muddy, out-of-focus way, they do know the essence of the melody. In such a case, you can go into the space and, with total trust, play four bars of the melody. No matter what it sounded like, you should take your hands off the instrument, return to the space ... put your hands on the instrument and let them play those four bars ... again remove your hands and let go, and so forth. Each time, without trying, you will experience more clarity, because you will be playing the same passage over and over. The key to this approach is removing the hands and letting go mentally. That means *being willing to play the passage sloppily, or even incorrectly*. The feeling of sure-handedness must be achieved at any cost (not that playing incorrectly is much of a price to pay for effortlessness – it just *seems that way*). Upon returning to the passage over and over again, you will experience a sense of your hands being magnetically drawn to better notes and rhythms, or to the correct notes and interpretation of the written piece. Each time it will become clearer and clearer. You aren't yet working on new or demanding material, but the material previously known to you is coming into greater focus.

Step Three is about doing what you can do and no more. As you get into this step, you may find your musical conception affected in interesting ways. Instead of playing tunes the way you think they should be played, you might naturally opt for the way you're ready to play them. For example, everyone thinks that *Cherokee** has to be played at a very fast tempo. Do you stop to ask yourself if you are ready to play so fast at that particular moment? Are you ever ready to play that tempo? Just as water seeks its own level, relaxation seeks its own tempo. Your feeling on that tune may seem so natural that it might persuade other musicians that this is a new way to play it. You might have unwittingly created a new conception for that tune. Isn't it ironic that the naturalness of the feeling could cause a

---

*Cherokee is another old standard song.

listener to think, "Wow, what a hip idea he had," when the strength was coming as a result of doing what was natural for you at that moment? Also, you don't always have the same abilities at all times. A tune might warrant a different conception at seven o'clock in the morning than at ten o'clock at night. If you're going with that flow, the tune might go through the same changes that your day went through, or even reflect those changes. Instead of people sensing your limitations, they might marvel at how many ways you can conceive of playing the same tune. If you obey your inner self too much, someone might call you a genius! The same is true when you play a week at a club. Different versions of the tunes are likely to develop naturally as the week goes on, but you might thwart the natural development by trying to do too much on the first night. These days, many players have so much trouble getting gigs that when they have one, they want to force the music to sound as if they had been touring for six weeks. The result is usually a lot of over-playing, or strained music. *The most honest way to play is to stay out of the way.* This is one of the essential teachings of Step Three. You may have heard this said by many great players in one way or another, but have you ever been able to take this knowledge to your instrument?

Step Three is the practice of just that: staying out of the way while playing the tune, and accepting what happens. In doing so, you may allow deeper feelings to find a voice; or, because there are no barriers between you and the inner self, you may be able to express pure consciousness, so that we may have a look inside ourselves. Kurt Vonnegut said about his friend, abstract expressionist painter, Syd Solomon:

"He meditates. He connects his hand and paintbrush to the deeper, quieter, more mysterious parts of his mind — and he paints pictures of what he sees and feels down there. — This accounts for the pleasurable shock of recognition we experience when we look at what he does."[1]

Build a bridge from the finite to the infinite. Face your

---

[1]Vonnegut, Kurt. *Palm Sunday, An Autobiographical Collage.* New York: Dell Publishing Co., 1981.

demons! Let yourself sound bad! Celebrate it! Like diving into the water, you may at first sink, but you always rise to the top and then float effortlessly. Go from a dry, intellectual and unsatisfying experience to a new, exciting ride every time you play. The depth of your playing may well change the course of your future, as you are developing an attractive light for others to follow. Just remember to be very gentle with yourself during this process. Don't think of it as some kind of test of your past achievements, or it will invalidate you in your own mind. Instead, think of it as the beginning of coming to terms with what's been holding you back, and taking powerful, positive steps to correct that and move forward. Be brave, be patient, and most of all, be loving to yourself throughout.

"When they leave behind the imperfections of the self, they dance.

Their minstrels play music from within; and whole oceans of passion foam on the crest of the waves."

— Rumi Jallaludin[2]

"If you forget yourself, you become the universe."

— Hakuin Ortegama[3]

[2]Rumi Jallaludin. *The Mathnavi.* [1260]. Translated by R. A. Nicholson. 6 vols. Cambridge: Cambridge University Press, 1934. Fragments translated by Daniel Liebert. Santa Fe: Source Books, 1981.
[3] *Zen Master Hakuin: Selected Writings.* [1748]. Translated by Philip Yampolsky. New York: Columbia University Press, 1971.

Chapter 20

Step Four

Ⓑy now, you will have built a foundation of effortlessness and detachment. In Step One, you learned to touch your instrument from that effortless space, to play a note or a few notes while allowing the connection to be made. In Step Two, you practiced staying in that space while your hands roamed around, making their own choices. You resisted the temptation to "organize" the material into musical ideas. Step Three showed you the absolute economy of what you can play in form, be it a tune or whatever. You were able to let your body take control and do only what it knows how to do. You also found that this was much less than you thought you could do. You might have found that meaningless, ill-fitting flourishes were replaced by real and meaningful phrases. Step Three showed you what you really knew and what was still in need of mastering.

After all that, the question naturally comes up: "If I'm to accept whatever wants to come out, then how do I improve on what I am playing?" Can one actually stay in the space while being absorbed in the rigors of practice? Obviously, I think so, or I wouldn't have written this book.

As stated earlier, mastery is not about being able to play something correctly most of the time, or even all of the time. Mastery is being able to play it perfectly every time *without thought*. Now that you're able to retain the awareness of "the inner space" while performing actions, achieving mastery over new technical things really becomes possible. "This state of unconsciousness is realized only when, completely empty and rid of the self, he becomes one with the perfecting of his technical skill."[1]

---

[1]Eugen Herrigel, *Zen In The Art Of Archery* p. 35.

Step Four requires you to take small samples of things you can't quite execute, and absorb them on a level of mastery. It combines the effortlessness of Step One and the freedom of movement of Step Two, and applies these to specific examples of things you can't do — familiarizing yourself with something rhythmic, harmonic, or melodic on such a deep level that it feels as though you are just wiggling your fingers.

This practicing must be very focused, very intentional. The length of time you practice must be limited to the length of time you can remain in the space. Then you must STOP! or you will compromise the deliberateness of the practice. In this way, five or ten minutes of practice is preferable to two hours of rambling.

This is important: *the player must be willing to put the instrument down often!* This could mean releasing the instrument after each repetition, if necessary. The drummer puts his sticks down, the horn player puts the horn on the floor or on a chair, the pianist takes his hands off the keyboard. Here again, the practice of releasing the instrument and starting again says that the player is not attached to the goal, though he patiently strives for it day after day. He will find that if he plays once or twice and releases the instrument, takes a deep breath and starts again, the very next time will be easier and more familiar, as the information "seeps in." Though he is drawn towards effort, by stopping, he retreats into the stillness and guides his technique into effortlessness. His ego will seduce him into trying harder, but *he should actually try less the next time.* Perfection is something you surrender to. It overcomes you. When ready to resume practicing, one should go in the opposite direction mentally. Instead of wanting to do better, the musician might even think, *"I hope I play it wrong!"* As weird as it sounds, such a thought may trick the mind into letting go, resulting in surprising ease of execution.

The objective is nothing less than complete perfection. When the passage is perfectly executed from the space, mastery has occurred. No matter how difficult the example seemed at the beginning, it is now performed with the mindlessness of using a fork. I cannot over-emphasize that although your practicing seems unbearably slow, your playing really takes off! That kind of concentration and infinite patience makes the act of playing feel like a release. You feel as if you were riding a bicycle with the wind at your back. It may seem as if *someone is playing for you while you're watching!* Don't judge your progress by daily measure, but notice improvement in your playing over time. More maneuverability, more freedom and more creativity will result.

In order to practice in this absolute space, the material must be absorbed in an exact way. You must limit the length of time, size of the example, and all parameters of the practice to *that which you can do from the space*. For this purpose, I have constructed a model of practicing that I call *The Learning Diamond*. It breaks your practicing down into four basic considerations:

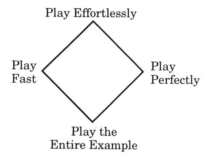

Play Effortlessly

Play Fast

Play Perfectly

Play the Entire Example

Play effortlessly - This one consideration is more important than the others. If the example isn't practiced from the effortless space, you can't be sure you've mastered it. So no matter what you are practicing, we will agree on this consideration. However, the other three corners of the square are interchangeable. That is to say, if you want to do any two of them, you have to sacrifice one of them. For example, if you are going to play the entire example perfectly and effortlessly, then you must sacrifice tempo: *don't play it fast.* You don't necessarily have to play it slow, either. Play it <u>*as slow as*</u>: as slow as needed to play it effortlessly and perfectly, while playing the whole thing.

If you want to play the exercise perfectly and very fast, and, of course, effortlessly, then you have to sacrifice the amount of it you play. In other words, *you can't play the whole example.* How much of it should you play? *As much as:* as much as you can play effortlessly, perfectly and very fast.

If you want to play the exercise from beginning to end very fast, and, as always, effortlessly, then you must sacrifice *playing it perfectly*. It may sound strange, but there is therapeutic value in letting your fingers rip on a difficult passage while playing many wrong notes. It gives the feeling of what effortless execution *will feel like*. Admittedly, this should only be done occasionally, but it does have a purpose.

If speed is not an issue, there may still be a tempo at which the passage needs to be played. In this case "playing in time" would replace the "playing fast" corner of the diamond.

The trickiest scenario is practicing something fast and perfectly, but not the whole example. If you're really in the space, the amount of the passage playable may be as little as one note. You may even find that playing the first two notes quickly requires effort. Achieve absolute mastery over the first note, then add the second note. Stay in the space and wait for the two notes to flow. Those two notes should feel as if they are being played automatically before you add a third. It is a feeling of perfect natural motion, like something you've done all you life. You will come to recognize when you are really "in there." You must stay very alert, very aware. People tend not to notice when the first two notes are not yet "in there." They are consumed with wanting to get it done, probably due to their fear of dying before they've mastered the passage! It is amazing how many little technical things surface to be mastered in the playing of just two notes. Remember that these two notes must be as easy and reliable as playing one (or using a fork). When you are on such firm ground, you may add the third note, and so on. You may want to stop after four or five notes and begin with fresh concentration on the sixth, connecting it to the previous four or five. By all means, do so. Through all of this, you often take your hands off the instrument and breathe into the space. You'll usually notice that progress has been made immediately following these "mini-breaks." If you lose patience for this kind of conscious approach, *you should stop.* This is true whether you like it or not, even if you've scheduled four hours for practicing; and have three hours and fifty-five minutes left. *Mastery will overtake you in the quickest possible fashion if your practicing is limited to only what you can do in that space!*

Your next practice should be a continuation of your last. If you were working on a passage and were up to the third note, then you should review those three notes to make sure that the absorption took place. If not, start over *as if you hadn't done it the first time!* If you find that you have absorbed those three notes, then go on to the forth note. This strings all your mini-practice sessions into one long practice, and removes the anxiety over what to practice. Always start where you left off. It's that simple. Ask yourself, "What was I practicing? Was it mastered?" Put your hands on the instrument and find out. If not, then you should start again on the same material. You should focus on only one thing to practice, as if nothing else existed in the music world. You may have two or three exercises: perhaps one rhythmic, one melodic and one harmonic exercise, or one to three short written passages. *The feeling that you should be practicing more should be ignored! Know that the level of concentration you are employing is changing your playing in the fastest possible way!* That is why learning to work from the space is so important: *you have to reach a zone where time is timeless and effort is effortless, and becoming great is not important!*

To summarize, the way you would practice under this system is to:

1) try it once, notice the glitch;

2) take your hands off the instrument;

3) take a deep breath and go back to the space;

4) approach the instrument with detachment again; and

5) *try less.*

Of all things, this last idea is the hardest to understand. How are you going to perfect the example by *trying less?* The less you try, the more you withdraw into the space, the more you enter a consciousness that feels as though your hands, embouchure or whatever, *are absorbing the lessons without thinking.* You are settling into the master-like consciousness of non-doership, and *watching it happen.* On the other hand by trying; (1) you are obscuring the reasons why you *have to try;* (2) you are covering up glitches that probably plague you in other situations; and (3) whatever you accomplish will be flawed and, therefore, *undone* later. If you can learn to stay in observation mode while your hands learn their choreography, they will show you the most efficient, most effortless way of executing the example. When in that state, *knowledge arises spontaneously.* Hence, there is no need to hold the body in any position, or even think of positioning. The body will surrender to the perfect position. People who do various physical therapies and disciplines may disagree, but I have found this to be quite true. By removing all anxiety-producing desires from the heart, all that's left is *perfection.*

Remember: to practice three corners of the Learning Diamond perfectly, one corner has to be sacrificed. And of the four corners, the one that is never sacrificed is *playing effortlessly.*

Examples of Things to Practice

To learn a great line, start with a great line. Transcribe it, or get it out of a book (there are so many now), or figure it out yourself. Then practice it by using the Learning Diamond to the point of mastery. After you master that line in one key, change the key or the line, and follow the same process carefully towards mastery. Work on the different lines and keys one at a time, maintaining the standard of excellence every time. All sorts of glitches will be exposed and remedied. Your playing will improve with every problem solved. There is nothing earth-shattering here. The question is not what to practice, which can be found everywhere, but *how to practice.* The radical idea is to stay with the example until it is effortlessly mastered. Then work on the next line until *that line sounds as good as the last.* You might work on lines for two years, but the good news is that *in only two years your lines will be great,* or at least vastly improved. Practicing the old way, it could take ten years, or not happen at all.

After each line is mastered, ask yourself, "Is my playing in general on that level yet?" If the answer is no, learn another line. If you stay with this method for as long as it takes, your ability to play great lines *will have to happen!* It's not a matter of talent. You'd have to have some sort of brain malfunction, something that actually inhibits learning, for it not to happen!

If you're a person who likes to work with music books, you can do that. However, don't think of the whole book when working with it. Instead, center on a certain page or a specific item that interests you while adopting the attitude that *nothing else in the book matters until that one item is mastered.* In this way you might very well study one book for twenty-five years if it has that much in it for you! Time doesn't matter, because you will be noticing more improvement than ever before. The practicing may lack instant gratification, but your overall progress will be undeniable. Don't we all have stacks of books that we've been meaning to tackle, but which instead sit on the shelf gathering dust? That is because we can't fathom the enormousness of the task. *All those books!* With this focused approach, you can center on one thing as a place to begin. You may feel exhilaration at having finally begun! Remember, the greatest musicians in jazz have not mastered most of the things in those books. They have mastered a few things and made a career out of playing them!

Some people have played tunes for years, but still haven't memorized many. This is a perfect example of overload. Your mind tells you that there are *so many tunes!* If you were to study the tunes one at a time with the approach described here, you simply wouldn't leave a composition until the task was complete. This experience would give you more confidence in your ability to memorize, and you would memorize more easily in the future.

The tune should be digested on all levels before moving on. The changes, scales and melody should come to you easily. How many of you have played certain tunes for twenty or thirty years and still play wrong changes or have trouble spots? Don't you think you're intelligent enough to straighten these things out after twenty years? The point is *that you don't!* As with other issues, you might think that this is the result of a lack of talent, but it is simply the result of trying to learn tunes in bulk. If you take them one at a time, *you will finally memorize tunes!* Some of you older musicians know exactly what I'm talking about. Wouldn't it be better to fix a few things once and for all, than be permanently disabled? Of course it would, but we are more comfortable with old habits than dealing with change.

For example, in *All the Things You Are**, you could isolate the II-V-I** in E major and practice until it was your most comfortable key. Then, when playing that tune, you would be one of the few musicians for whom that was the easiest part of the tune! It is the inability to focus that causes the same dysfunction year after year.

The steps to mastery are simple, but not easy to follow because the mind plays tricks on you. For example, practicing a single idea for one year feels like a lifetime, and you succumb to the illusion that no progress is being made. In reality, you might be progressing for the first time in a long time, but it doesn't feel like it, because you're not changing the direction of the practice every few weeks. Although it may take a long time to perfect one item, you will notice that the focus and patience you've exhibited has clearly improved your playing, even before the first example is mastered. Many of my students told me that even though they were practicing less than ever, their playing had improved in areas that they had almost given up on. Let me be clear about this: I am not advising anyone to only practice a little bit; I am just saying that exhausting your patience, focus, and thoroughness is counter-productive. If you can develop your inner space and study from there, you will do

---

**All the Things You Are* is another standard.
**"II-V-I" is a basic chord progression or succession of chords used in jazz.

your best work, and the time spent in that concentrated state *will increase*. Go for that depth, and don't rate the practice in measurements of time. Try not to even be aware of the time. The key to good practicing is having a laser-like focus on the material, and not leaving it until your playing has derived the full benefits. These are the fruits of Step Four.

The mind; ah, the blessed mind! It will talk to you during this process. It will tell you, "Come on! We gotta move on. We're wasting so much time!" But look at it rationally. You have practiced things in the past and seen little or no improvement. This is because you didn't stay with it long enough for the information to penetrate. If you practiced something for two weeks and didn't see much improvement but moved on, *didn't you truly waste your time?* The only way you don't waste time is by moving toward your goal until it is accomplished. You are not wasting your time as long as you *stay with it!*

If you weren't so concerned about your level of playing, you'd hang in for as long as it took. It would be like a hobby. That's why this book stresses again and again developing a detachment to what you're doing while you are doing it. However, it is so easy to become discouraged. All you need is one night when you didn't play what you wanted to hear, and the ego says, "Screw it! It's not happening." Again and again, this needs to be said: you probably cannot develop this level of patience if you are *vain about your playing!*

If you are practicing a certain line on a certain chord change, this passive way of practicing will let the sound of that chord and scale seep in, and you will become familiar with the sound on a very intimate level. That is tantamount to deep ear-training, meditating on a sound so deeply that you now recognize it whenever you hear it. I've had many students tell me that in the process of working on an example to achieve technical ease, they noticed for the first time that they could really hear what others were playing; they could recognize what they were practicing when it showed up in another player's solo. That is why I try to center the linear exercises around II-V-I for relatively new people. A novice may think that there is so much to learn to hear that he becomes blocked and afraid. But if he really absorbs II-V-I, he will hear much more of what's being played. This gives him a new confidence, like becoming a member of a club that previously wouldn't have him. As a result of such positive programming, subsequent things go better. If you find that you have a good command over this progression, then it is truly time to look at other progressions, perhaps *Giant Steps** or some other post-bebop progression. The next step might be tunes that are increasingly sophisticated in one way or another, or even the music of other cultures. You'll find that the melodic lessons you learn by studying II-V-I's will apply, and you will not be hampered in your study of newer chords. The ability to tastefully blow on the II-V-I progression will give you the necessary skills for employability, since this is still the language most musicians speak. It allows you to get gigs and "get in the life." It will attract other players to you. You will form unions with them and eventually find your own sound together. Speaking intelligently on II-V-I will allow you to take your musical journey to the next level through sessions, gigs and collaborations. The basic components to be mastered, as I've stated before, are 4/4 time, 3/4 time, the II-V-I progression, rhythm and time, and four and eight bar phrases. Mastery of these issues will take you very far indeed!

The greats in our music do not totally improvise from moment to moment. They are actually playing rehearsed lines and improvising their juxtaposition. Like any human being, a master gets in the habit of using the same phrases. This doesn't sound redundant in his hands, but identifies his voice.

Mastering the basic mechanics of "inside" jazz is only a suggestion. It maximizes your compatibility with the greatest amount of players at the beginning of your career. However, you may want to go your own way from the start, perhaps identifying with more exotic elements in music. Your path may be ethnic, esoteric, spiritual or hedonistic, and that's okay, because music

---

Giant Steps is one of John Coltrane's most famous compositions.

is the haven for all of that. Even anger has beauty and color when expressed in musical tone. Be prepared, however, for the possibility of having a tougher road to travel. You will have to be shown where your avenues of expression lie and be united with kindred spirits by unseen forces. In that case, it is even more important to have a connection to the divine or intuitive self. You might need guidance from within to carry you through possible bleak times and help you make choices. Contemplate on the deepest level why you are playing music and what you love most in music.

In any case, your music will require learning of some kind. Whether it be classical or any other style, you will have to study. Step Four is the most conscious, perfection-oriented method of practice you could adopt. Its intention is nothing less than mastery. Mastery is the standard to achieve over more and more material. It would be difficult to imagine students in most cases being able to practice on this level without the foundation of the first three steps. I'm sure there are some people that fall into deep concentration naturally, but most of us have to be led out of the mediocre funk we've been taught to identify with. The first three steps will do that.

Indeed, this standard of mastery resembles a process more common in other cultures. Studying with the masters of those traditions, one had better not be in a hurry, because the teacher doesn't allow one to move on until the goal at that level has been achieved. Also, in those traditions, *the teacher is a master!* That is often not the case in the West.

As I said before, anyone can tell you what to practice, but there is almost no guidance as to how to practice. Some teachers let you move on regardless of how poorly you've learned the last lesson, and that standard becomes encoded in your subconscious. It's time to change now. These four steps are designed to let you grow into mastery *in your own time.* Mastery is achievable if you'll wait for it.

At this point in my clinics, many students have mentioned that they know that what I'm saying is absolutely true — that they practice too much material, or don't stay with it long enough, or don't practice at all because they are overwhelmed for the reasons I have identified. The problem, they say, is that they can't stop everything they are doing in the real world and just practice one thing. They have juries (there's that *word* again!) or ensembles for which to prepare. Those who are out of school complain that they have gigs to prepare for or jobs that take all their time. I work with students who are teachers and even heads of music departments, and they say that they can't do it because they are too busy teaching or administrating. It is a problem that I acknowledge, and there is an answer.

You must have a "secret compartment" in your day of five, ten or twenty minutes. It could be several pockets of five minutes each. These compartments are reserved only for practicing from the effortless space. If you are working on Steps One, Two or Three, then these times are reserved for that. If you have decided on a Step Four exercise, then you would get into the space and consciously work on that for a small length of time. After those few minutes, you could close that secret compartment and move on through the other realities of your day. In this way, you will be effecting fundamental changes in your playing that will cause other things in your musical life to improve.

Don't forget that the weak aspects of your game, so to speak, will hamper your musical activities. For example, if you don't read music very well, that will affect the type of gigs you can take. If your rhythm or time is bad, every rehearsal or gig will bring unwanted adventure. Wouldn't it be great if, in your secret compartment, you were mastering one rhythmic exercise after another and feeling all your rhythm improve?

You can't practice everything on this level — there just isn't enough time. Many things come up in your career that require you to practice as quickly as possible and hope for the best. You cannot — repeat — *CANNOT consciously force this focus in your playing or practicing.* The mind creates a funny twist on the situation, and you start *trying not to try,* and get caught in the middle. It's Hell! The results are usually disastrous, and will scare you into diluting the methods greatly.

170

Enter your secret compartment and for that time, let all deadlines and pressures cease to be. The only thing that matters is the quality of your focus and concentration. The superior concentration you build will bleed into your gigs and other practice responsibilities. You will notice, after some time, that even when you're not practicing in the space, you are almost in it anyway. Even though you have to learn something on deadline, you are much more focused while doing it and much more successful in absorbing what you're practicing. Eventually, there will be no difference in states of mind. To approach your instrument for any reason will inspire calm, focus, inner connection and great concentration.

Chapter 21
An Afterthought

*J*ust as impatience upsets concentration, success may also lead to your undoing. The "hit" you get from periodic "jumps" in your playing level may throw your inner state out of whack. You'll be thinking, "Yeah, I've really got it now! Let's forget all this Zen stuff and really burn!"

Alas, the ego will have tricked you once again, and your practicing will decay into the ordinary. It's okay for this to happen. In a sense, it has to happen. You will mature in this process by your own experience: losing patience, forsaking the space in frustration, or being unable to focus because of your sudden success. After you realize that everything has again become dry, you will become willing to review the steps and re-enter the space. You may think you've blown it or lost time, but you will have been following the same pattern everyone does in trying to learn. Your own experience will confirm the wisdom of the process every time you return to it. You will regain your center and feel connected again. Then, just when you think you understand it all, it will change again, and you will feel more bewildered than ever. You will go through this cycle many times: holding the space, losing the space, relishing the space, hating the space.The more times you go around, the more hip you become to the game. It is a game or a play, and if you understand that, you can witness all the phases you go through with more compassion.

Understand that progress is not linear. It zig-zags: "two steps forward, one step back." This happens with anything you practice. However, you can view a step backwards as an opportunity to start over. This is always a blessing in disguise. Plodding on the same path drives it deeper into the subconscious, making it more *unconscious,* like breathing. Imagine drawing lines in the sand with your foot. Which is progress — drawing new lines, or dragging your foot over the same line? The former results in more lines, which seems like progress – but do those lines last, or do they blow away with the first breeze? In the latter approach, the line *gets deeper.* The progress achieved is more long-lasting.

As I said before, you can free your mind from superficial thoughts by surrendering the need to accomplish anything when practicing. Play with the thought that it is not necessary to be a great player. If you don't really feel that this is true, then just pretend that it is. I know, of course, that you care. I care, but as I'm about to practice or play, I give myself the message that nothing matters. Imposing fewer conditions on your practicing disarms the ego and brings you into the moment.

Imposing fewer conditions on your playing also frees you to rise to the occasion. A CD I recorded with Joe Lovano called *Universal Language* is a good case in point. It was my first time playing with the two great icons of jazz, bassist Charlie Haden and drummer Jack DeJohnette.The first fear I had was that Jack, Charlie and Joe, being total road warriors, would be "burning" from continuous touring. At that time, I had had a long layoff between tours, which included a lot of talking, teaching and arranging, but not much playing. In fear mode, I might have spent the weekend practicing Joe's pieces furiously, trying to "burn" right there in my home. In other words, I would be trying to simulate the moment when I would be playing with these guys. The worst thing that could have happened is that *I would be burning!* That would have raised my expectations about achieving the same level at the recording. Instead, I sat down at the piano for many short periods, going into the space and letting my hand hover around the notes and tonalities it wanted to play, never worrying about finishing a thought or playing well at all. I would calmly look over Joe's tunes and let my fingers lightly move over the notes, but never simulating the performance. I knew that my strength could come from nothing tangible, but entirely from within. The point is, my practice consisted entirely of *connecting with the inner self.* I knew that that connection was more important than the music!

When I got to the studio, I was aware of wanting Haden and DeJohnette to like me. I was even conscious of wanting to say something deep and profound so that everyone would respect me as a deep thinker. However, having practiced witness-consciousness for quite a while, I observed that urge and kept relatively quiet.

When we went into the studio to play, DeJohnette and I were placed on either side of a wall with a window. I was facing him with about fifteen feet between us. With musicians like Charlie and Jack, the temptation to think of the great Keith Jarrett is strong, as they had both been members of Jarrett's historic groups at different times. I realized that thinking of that was a losing proposition. Instead of succumbing to the urgings of the mind, I went into the space I had honored in myself all weekend, the space I have now dedicated my life to, and stared at Jack with an in-drawn awareness while *my hands played the music.*

Later, when we listened back to the track, I realized that everything had happened that I had wanted to happen. I was burning on the level of the other guys, as if I was as road-ripe as they were. I had my own voice and could feel my heart in the music. The musicians reacted to my playing in the way that my ego had originally craved. For me, it was a ringing endorsement of the life I have chosen and the method I have embraced.

These exercises never stop working. It is we who stop giving ourselves to the practice. As I said, a little success satiates us, and we stop giving. If you do Step One with all your heart, you will reach great levels of focus. Once you reach it, you will not remember what you were giving to it, but only the results that were created. The next time you do Step One, you may say to the exercise, "Come on, get me high again," and you will forget to give everything you have to the experience. You will have expectations and, therefore, not be open to how the exercise might manifest that particular time. Then you will complain that "it's not working." It's not that it isn't working; it's that *you stopped giving!* You can become lazy and careless as you attain the fruits of this practice and desire slips away. Don't identify with success or failure.

When you give yourself to the space, you get much in return, so *don't forget to give as much as you can!* Another paradox: *the way to get high is by giving.* It takes quite a few times around the block before you realize this. When the experience leaves you, *ask for the willingness to give yourself again,* and it will be granted. If you return with an open, willing heart, you go right back to the pot of gold. Through humility, you become teachable again. When you lose the way, go back to the practices; not just these practices, but whatever you discover for yourself, and rededicate yourself to surrender. That wonderful energy returns, convincing you that you are on the right path.

When you do lose the space, the thing to do is *go back to Step One.* Don't be afraid to start all over. Do it with great joy. It is not really starting over, but turning a page. Steps Two and Three would also be good to review, but Step One is to music what meditation is to a spiritual path: a renewal, a reaffirmation and a deepening of commitment and understanding. It puts you in much greater balance to do Step Four. When you lose your way, take one week and practice Step One, and perhaps Two, with all the heart and focus you can summon. The feeling will return, and that feeling is almost more desirable than playing itself. In fact, for me, it *is* more desirable. It brings the glow back into my playing and practicing, and I am grateful for it. You really won't want to return to Step One, but whenever you've lost patience for the whole process, it means that the process itself needs some watering at the root. If you don't keep going back to the root, you will probably lose this process. When you are not centered, the exercises become boring, and you quit. I have taught many students over the last ten years, and I've seen how it goes. Believe me, *you need to go back to Step One.*

Five Minute Technique

As I pointed out before, some people don't practice unless they can spend two or three hours at it. Since they often don't have that amount of time, they don't practice. Some do have the time but are overwhelmed by the thought of it all. Here is a little mental trick to get you going. Just tell yourself that *you are only going to practice for five minutes.* Every time you begin, be sure to stop after five minutes, regardless of what's been accomplished. You'll find that if you think "It's only five minutes," then it will be easy to start. The problem is often not practicing, *but starting.* Once you've started, you may want to continue, but let your intention be only five minutes. You can always deal with that. Without your noticing, five minutes becomes ten, ten becomes twenty, and so on. However once you start expecting longer periods, *you may stop practicing again!* That feeling of being overwhelmed will return. Always make it five, and consider any more to be a bonus. As I expressed it earlier, five minutes can be most useful indeed. You can reach your goal with surprising efficiency through a series of five-minute practices. You just need a clear idea of what you're going to focus on.

Mildred Chase writes about the power of a short practice in her book, *Just Being At The Piano:* "I no longer feel tormented as I used to when I am unable to fit in my hours of practice. Now even if I have only fifteen minutes at the piano on an extremely busy day, if I can reach this state of harmony in my playing even briefly, I leave the instrument knowing that I have experienced the heightened moment, and to touch on it will nourish the rest of the day."[1]

Through these precious moments of perfect action, you delineate this clear concentration from all other states you experience in your day. That state will expand and the feeling of perfection will become increasingly familiar. As you continue practicing, it will feel less like an attitude adjustment, and more like the "real you." The less you react to the change, the more

---

[1]Chase, Mildred, *Just Being at the Piano.* Berkeley: Creative Arts Books.

natural it becomes ... and it all grows together.

When you feel as though you've lost it, wave it goodbye with gratitude, calmly assured that it will return to you again soon, like a celestial visitor with you being the devoted host. William Blake said it beautifully:

He who binds to himself a joy

Doth the winged life destroy;

But he who kisses the joy as it flies

Lives in Eternity's sunrise.[2]

You never really lose it, you know. It is who you really are. It is the "real you." All your days will be filled with effortless action, masterful work, blessed detachment. You will have achieved your goal while being less attached to it than you could have ever imagined.

"He who loves does not think about his own life ... Love is the very marrow of beings ... Love will open the door ... Go forward then without fear. Forsake childish things and, above all, take courage." [3]

---

[2]William Blake. "The Pickering Manuscript" in *Blake, Complete Writings*. Edited by Geoffrey Keynes, Oxford: Oxford University Press, 1989.
[3]"Conference of the Birds" by Sufi poet and mystic, Attar.

Chapter 22

Meditation #3: I Am Great, I Am A Master

(Please listen to Meditation #3 on CD)

Sit and relax. When you do these meditations without the book, you should also close your eyes. Breathe in and let this be like your first meditation. Imagine looking at your life with joy, anticipation and excitement, because you don't know what's coming. As you accept whatever comes, your life becomes truly exciting. The music becomes truly exciting. Breathe that idea in ... Breathe it in ... *deeper than you want to* ... Breathe through all your resistance now ... Breathe through the shell of your ego. As powerful as the ego seems, it cannot withstand the power of a good deep breath, so ... breathe deeply ... It is so simple ... that is why we always miss it!

Right now, let's rejoice in the simplicity of it all. ... How simple it is to play ... how simple it is to create ... how simple it is to live and ... *breathe*. Let yourself realize how little we really need ...

And now breathe in this thought as if for the first time ... *I am great* ... Just let that thought swim around your head. *I am a master* ... *I am great.* Let it swim around your head like a fish in a fish bowl ... and swim down through your neck and shoulders ... and down your spine and through your chest and stomach ... and through your arms and hands ... these two thoughts ... *I am great* ... *I am a master* ...

You have nothing to lose by surrendering to that thought completely ... could it possibly serve you more to think ... *I am not a master* ... *I am not great* ...?

In what way does that serve you? ... And yet, for many, it can be more comfortable to think that, than to just go for this thought: ... *I am great* ... *I am a master* ... *I am great* ... *I am a master* ...

I am great ... I am a master ... The Infinite Force of the universe is waiting for us to realize ... we don't have to kill ... we don't have to conquer ... we don't have to do anything ... *we are great! ... we are masters ...* See the day when everyone walks the earth ... firm in the knowledge that ... *they are masters! ...* But now ... for you ... let's practice seeing ourselves as masters ... today.

I am great ... I am a master ...

Breathe that in as you relax your face ... your mouth ... your tongue ... throat ... relax your ears ... widen the canals in your ears ... so wide that your head disappears!

I am great ... I am a master ...

Feel your eyes ... ears ... nose ... and throat widen.

I am great ... I am a master ...

Feel your neck and shoulders melt into effortless relaxation ... a warm melting feeling that moves down into your upper back ... your chest ... ribcage ... your heart ... liver and kidneys ... all your inner organs ... picture your intestines relaxing and expanding, widening until your stomach disappears ... and in the pit of your stomach, put this thought ...

I am great ... I am a master ...

Focus on your spine ... feel every vertebra ... imagine your spine lengthening now and reaching up to the sky! You're not stretching it, your spine is stretching you, reaching up higher and higher ... feel the space between each vertebra getting wider ... feel a laser of light shooting into your head and down your spine ... your spine looks like a lightning rod, burning with light! ... Imagine now that the light in your spine has exploded and your whole upper body has disappeared ... all that exists where your upper body used to be is a blinding light ... See an incredible explosion of light! ... The light explodes and across the sky is written in light ... blazing light ...

I am great ... I am a master ...

And now that light goes shooting into your buttocks and legs ... and your knees and ankles and feet ... warming every cell ... burning every cell ... exploding every cell! ... All pains ... all illness ... burned away by the brilliance of this light. ... The light is now shooting into your arms, elbows and hands ... exploding every cell ... as more and more of your body disappears ... and all there is is blazing light ... you are that blazing light! ... breathe in that light ... deeply ... and the words you can see inscribed in that light ...

I am great ... I am a master ...

Say this in your mind:

I now dedicate my life to realizing ... *I am great ... I am a master ...*

Every note I play will sing ... *I am great ... I am a master ...*

Every piece I compose will be a celebration of the truth ... *We are all great ... We are all masters ...*

And every time we hear your music, we will feel great ... we will feel like masters ... Your music will spread the realization that we all are masters.

You don't have to worry about how you will achieve this, or how you will manipulate everyone into believing it ... you're simply programming yourself into thinking ... *I am great ... I am a master ...*

Take this message into the depths of your being ... ignore all other messages ... keep reaffirming ... *I am great ... I am a master ...*

Other thoughts have limited value ... you may say thank you for those thoughts ... you don't have to fear those thoughts .... thank you for sharing ... but the truth is ... *I am great ... I am a master ...*

If you still feel resistance to that thought, ask yourself, "Why would I possibly want to resist that thought? What would I have to gain by denying that thought?" That is worth contemplating. What do you gain by proving that thought to be wrong! Even if you can do it ... what would you gain?

So go for it ... one more time ...

I am great ... I am a master ...

When you see the sun, see your own greatness ... when you see your reflection on the water, feel your own mastery ... look at other people and see nothing but masters around you ... it will only be to the good ... learn not to view them competitively, but celebrate their greatness ... honor the masters around you ... celebrate the greatness around you and that greatness will reflect back to you ... You'll have negative thoughts, you'll trip and fall along the way, we know that ... but keep reaffirming ... at every opportunity ... at every glimmer of willingness ... *I am great ... I am a master ...*

I am great ... I am a master ...

You may experience many more cloudy moments than sunny moments, but whenever there is the slightest hole in the clouds and the sun can peek through ... reaffirm ...

I am great ... I am a master ...

Be open to any moment in which you are willing to accept the truth ...

Take a very deep breath ... then take five more and as you inhale, inhale the thought ... *I am great ... I am a master ...* and exhale any imperfection or negative thought you have about your self ...

I am great ... I am a master ...

I am great ... I am a master ...

I am great ... I am a master ...

I am great ... I am a master ...

Chapter 23
Stretching The Form

$\mathcal{T}$he pinnacle of development in a human being is the full expression of his animal, intellectual, and spiritual nature. John Coltrane exemplified this ideal as a musician. I think he reached the apex of all three through music. His animal nature was expressed on the bandstand. He would be soaked in sweat as he played incredibly long and burning solos. Had his intellect been active at that moment, it would have surely drained his energy. Trane attacked the tune like a cat stalking prey, with total single-mindedness.

However, his intellectual contribution to the music is undeniable. It is well-documented that he revolutionized the way the tenor saxophone is played. His lines constituted a new way of playing on and stretching chord progressions. Other saxophonists felt that they had to relearn their horns. With the invention of tunes like *Giant Steps* and *Countdown*, he actually gave us a new chord progression to deal with. All instrumentalists found themselves practicing a new dance step. How many players have had that effect on the entire community?

As for the spiritual, he was the most notable of the musicians of his time to bring African awareness to jazz. Along with Elvin Jones and others, he re-instituted the 12/8 rhythm inherent in traditional African music. Late in his life, he had forsook all drugs for the austerity of a spiritual path. His last quest was for the recognition of his inner being. I've talked to a few musicians who played with or hung out with him, and they've all said the same thing; that being with him was like being around a messianic figure. He evidently radiated that level of spirituality. All those who came in contact with him tended to live more in that awareness. He was like a lamp that lit other lamps. A musician can have that effect on people. Hazrat Inayat Khan said. "He who gradually progresses along the path of music, in the end attains the highest perfection."[1]

I can't promise you that if you practice Step One you'll inspire people to such levels, but you'll become a deeper person and a deeper musician as you move beyond shallow goals and closer to the divinity within you.

John Coltrane stretched the form of his life as well. He is a shining example of working on oneself, of changing and growing. He searched through heroin to psychedelics and finally found God before he died. Trane's path was a classic struggle to discover Self, to be a master of the Self.

When I made the decision to go to school on myself, a wonderful process evolved over a ten-year period. From practicing the effortless approach to piano, I had realized that it took ten years to really absorb a good lesson. This was an advantage as I didn't expect things to change overnight. That's not to say that I wasn't constantly impatient with myself, but knowing the time it takes helped me not to give up.

As I changed my conception of myself, outer results in my life also changed. Since then, many good things have continued to happen, and I am becoming more and more successful at what I do. If you ask me what changed, what did I do, whom did I call, to bring about this success, I can only reply, "Nothing." Nothing externally — but the new inroads I made in my belief structure preceded the outward changes and, in my mind, are absolutely responsible for everything. Begin your new programming now, have patience, and the seeds will grow into new inner and outer gifts.

In his book, *The Path Of Least Resistance*, Robert Fritz writes, "Once a structure exists, energy moves through that structure by the path of least resistance. In other words, *energy moves where it is easiest to go*." That explains the recurring failures that I have experienced in my life. Failure and despair were *the path of least resistance!*

---

[1]Hazrat Inayat Khan, *The Sufi Message*, p. 53.

I recently read a quote by Samuel Smiles that inspired me greatly. It said:

Sow an act, reap a habit,
sow a habit, reap a character,
sow a character, reap a destiny.

If you are building new patterns of success in your life, BE PATIENT. There is a time delay between planting new messages and their coming into fruition. A farmer does not go into his fields to tug on the shoots of his crops. He knows that growth happens in its own time.

During the middle and late eighties, I started to practice new patterns of thought that would eventually yield the successful results I had craved all my life. When new opportunities came my way, I maintained my interest in self-improvement, higher consciousness and growth in general, and those opportunities came to fruition.

I then knew that the curse was finally over! I could attract abundance and success into my life! Lo and behold, it works! I'm functional! I can learn!

My first big band chart took a year-and-a-half to complete, because I could only work on it for little bits at a time, when the right drug was available. Then I wouldn't write for weeks. In 1993, I proved to myself that a "new me" had been created by writing eleven big band charts – doing it on computer while learning the computer program. I worked ten or twelve hours a day for many days. That kind of concentration would have been impossible for me a few years earlier. That reward is the fruit of my labor on myself. Spiritual development had brought with it mental development in the form of concentration. Now I believe that there is no limit to how far I can go. The greatest thing is that *I am detaching from the results more and more.*

I became particularly aware of how deep my commitment to my spirit had become on one occasion when, while meditating, I received a call from a great musician for a great gig. I accepted it, put down the phone, and went back to my meditation as if nothing had happened. In previous days, my meditation would have been ruined as my mind, stimulated by the gig, would have raced. But instead I was just slightly annoyed that my meditation had been interrupted. That's a stretch!

Chapter 24

The Spiritual (Reprise)

*O*nce, I went away to a place of worship and meditation. Bowing was very common there. It was part of the practice. I thought it to be very weird, and I had trouble with bowing to anyone or anything. After awhile, I thought to myself, "You know, I paid a lot of money to be here, and if I don't get this, I don't want it to be because of something I didn't do!" I could see someone asking me later, "How did you like it?"and I would say, "It wasn't too great for me." "Well, did you bow?" "Well, uh, no," then they would say, "Ah, too bad! That's why you didn't get it." *I didn't want them to have any excuses.* So I proceeded to get my money's worth. If they bowed, I bowed; if they sang, I sang; if they prayed, I prayed. And a funny thing happened: I started to really dig bowing! Just the humble act of bowing started to feel more and more freeing. It felt good to be down there!

I became a bowing fool! I would go to rooms and bow to everything in sight. It felt as though I were freeing myself of some constriction, my ego. I didn't know where this was going, but I knew I felt great.

When I left, I was happy I had done it, and thought that maybe I'd come back again sometime and cool out this way. But I felt the real fruits when I returned home. It happened that I had a gig in New York City that night after not playing for awhile, and I went straight there. I'll never forget this experience. It was at Zinno's, a restaurant-jazz club that features piano and bass duos, and I was playing with Rufus Reid, a great jazz bassist. We were about to play for a week there, and I hadn't played for two weeks. I didn't know what to expect, but I felt so good that I couldn't imagine any problem. I sat down on the piano bench, put my hands on the piano, and instinctively *I bowed.* As I did this, I lovingly descended into the sweetest concentration I've ever known. I was receiving everything with gratitude, and the sound filled me with ecstasy. We played *My Romance** just simply and soulfully. I think we were both swaying back and forth as we played. It was a very profound experience for me, and I suddenly knew what that experience was all about. Just as the players in the forties and fifties had descended into the heroin state, I descended into a *state of grace*. When I bowed, I received everything, and I stayed in that bow for the whole tune. When it was over, I remained in this state a while longer, when I opened my eyes, I looked up at Rufus, and he was just hanging on his bass and swaying back and forth. He looked just like all the people in this place I had just been at. With eyes wide, he said in an intoxicated voice, "This is going to be fun, isn't it?" With equal intoxication, I nodded, yes. This was another of many experiences I've had that prove to me, beyond the shadow of a doubt, that *surrender is the greatest practice*. Through surrender, you will receive more than you ever dreamed of!

The only thing to add to this story is that later in the week, the feeling wore off. The gig became merely about good piano playing, and less about bowing. Something had worn off, but the desire to have that experience again burned in me brighter than ever. Having experiences like that makes you more thirsty for the inner nectar.

Many people assume that if you play music, your life has meaning; but many of us who play know that that's not necessarily true. Once I was talking to a jazz musician, who shall remain anonymous because he is famous. He had just come from a dinner, attended by some other great jazz musicians. It was a male bonding kind of dinner as they talked about their fathers, their careers, and their feelings. He told me something that was very revealing. Even though they were all great players and very successful, what did it all mean? I could really identify with the question, and I felt compassion for him. I didn't say anything, though I had an answer in my mind. The answer could

---

My Romance is a jazz standard.

be that nothing really does have meaning, no matter how much success you achieve, no matter how much of a master you become at what you do, if you do not offer it up to the divine power — God, if you like. Without the desire to know this part of myself, or my *true Self*, I would be groping for meaning at every second. It would be very hard to please me, no matter how good things were going. I am grateful for the pain that led to the pursuit of a higher Self.

Every spiritual teaching confirms that *it is better to give than to receive*. This is a well-known but little-followed teaching. By giving as much as you can to something, you become a channel to receive. The Christian bible also says, "I do not speak on my own authority, but the Father who dwells in me does his work."[1] I feel the same way about my solos. Whether you believe in the Father or not, this is the principle of effortless action: *Let the higher power play the music!*

Don't let the light of your search dim. Take a course, or a workshop, or surround yourself with people who are fighting the same battle as you are. Take big leaps when necessary to restore your willingness to continue on the path. When your mind won't let you go, you may need the strength of a group. When people congregate, they can accomplish more than individuals sitting alone. A hip lick I heard is, "An addict alone is in bad company." How true that is! And remember, we are all addicts in the sense that we are addicted to our limited vision of ourselves.

Be open to the possibility that rituals can restore your power. Rituals are the indispensable tool for nurturing our higher selves. Society has become weaker for lack of them. Many people are now seeking rituals to recover their lost identities. Musicians should not ignore society's search but take the lead, as in former times. You can make a ritual out of Step One, for example. Wear ceremonial garb, silks perhaps, or light candles, and seek out ways to increase the grace with which you surrender. In this way, you can prevent the decay of its meaning.

---

[1] Revised Standard Bible, John 14:10b.

Once I was asked, "What is the next stage of evolution in music for the next century?" My answer was that the evolution of music is not the issue. It is the evolution of the musician that's most important. The artist must take his rightful place in society as a teacher, metaphysician and visionary. By alchemistic processes, base metal is turned into gold. Similarly, we human beings may be transformed into gods and goddesses. Ask for this change to occur in your life.

"The harp gives forth murmurous music; and the dance goes on without hands and feet. It is played without fingers, it is heard without ears; for He is the ear; and He is the listener."

— Kabir[2]

"I played the Vina until my heart turned into this very instrument; then I offered this instrument to the divine musician, the only musician existing. Since then I have become His flute; and when he chooses, He plays his music. The people give me credit for this music, which is in reality not due to me but to the musician who plays his own instrument."

— Hazrat Inayat Khan[3]

Joke

There were two monks in a monastery doing their daily rituals. They were about to bow to their deity. One got on his knees and said, "Oh master, I am nothing, I don't exist, all there is is You." The next monk bowed down even lower and said, "Oh great one, I am less than nothing! I don't exist and I never did. You are all there is!" In the corner, a janitor was sweeping the temple and watching the monks. He thought to himself, "Hmmm, that looks pretty good! I think I'll try that." He walked over to the deity and bowed while the monks watched him. He said, "Oh mighty one, I too am nothing, you are everything." As the two monks looked on with disdain, one said to the other, "Humph! How dare he! *Look who thinks he's nothing!"*

Don't forget to renew your humility!

---

[2]Kabir, a fifteenth century poet-saint in India who worked as a weaver in Benares.
[3]Hazrat Inayat Khan, *The Sufi Message-Preface.*

Meditation #4: One Final Meditation

(Please listen to Meditation #4 on CD)

$\mathcal{T}$ake a long deep breath. Say thank you for that breath. Take another deep breath and learn the dance of your mind. Feel relaxation come into you now from the top of your head. Feel love and relaxation enter slowly and gently from the top of your head ... and melting down your face and dripping into your ears ... and filling your eyes ... filling your nostrils ... and filling your throat ... just simple love ... and relaxation ... filling your neck ... filling your shoulders ... your chest and your upper back ... filling your lower back and stomach. Feel this love and relaxation drip down into your heart ... and kidneys ... feel it bellowing in your lungs ... deep inhalations ... of love and relaxation ... deep exhalations ... of love and relaxation ... feel it melting down into your arms and hands ... melting your wrists ... down into your hips ... thighs ... knees ... calves ... ankles ... and feet ... Imagine now that you are only love and relaxation ... that's all that's left ... this job of burning away the ego seems tricky ... but imagine it is the simplest thing in the world to do ... don't focus on its trickiness ... reaffirm ... *I become love and light easily ... I become my higher Self easily ... I am perfection and mastery ... naturally ... I am a master ... I cannot lose that ... I am a master ... I can only pretend I'm not ...* turn it around ... the reality is ... *I am a master ...* the pretense is ... *I am not ...* breathe in ... *I am a master ...* your ego says ... no, no more, not even one more time! I can't stand it anymore! ... and you say, "Well, just one more time" ... *I am a master! ... just another moment ... I am a master ... I am ...*

I wish you all the outer and inner success that you can handle. I salute you as gods and goddesses, and I wish you effortless mastery in your life and in your music.

Kenny Werner

Kenny Werner

Often gives workshops
and concerts around the world

There will be events planned
and materials available to help
people practice the techniques and
realize the goals presented in this book.
If you would like to be on his mailing list,
please fill in your name and address, fax number,
and/or email address and send it to:

Kenny Werner
P.O. Box 536
Scotch Plains, N.J. 07076-0536

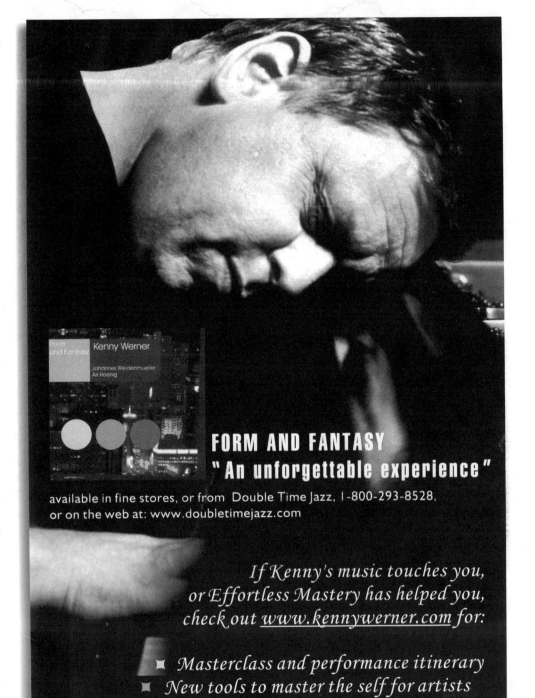

FORM AND FANTASY
"An unforgettable experience"

available in fine stores, or from Double Time Jazz, 1-800-293-8528, or on the web at: www.doubletimejazz.com

If Kenny's music touches you,
or Effortless Mastery has helped you,
check out www.kennywerner.com for:

- *Masterclass and performance itinerary*
- *New tools to master the self for artists*
- *Updated thoughts on Effortless Mastery*